Plato's Trial and Death of Socrates

By Plato

Table of Contents

Introduction

Of all writers of speculative philosophy, both ancient and modern, there is probably no one who has attained so eminent a position as Plato. What Homer was to Epic poetry, what Cicero and Demosthenes were to oratory, and what Shakespeare was to the drama of England, Plato was to ancient philosophy, not unapproachable nor unapproached, but possessing an inexplicable but unquestioned supremacy.

The authentic records of his life are meager, and much that has been written concerning him is of a speculative nature. He was born at Athens in the year 427 B.C. His father's name was Ariston, and his mother's family, which claimed its descent from Solon, included among its members many Athenian notables, among whom was Oritias, one of the thirty tyrants.

In his early youth Plato applied himself to poetry and painting, both of which pursuits he relinquished to become the disciple and follower of Socrates. It is said that his name was originally Aristocles, but that it was changed to Plato on account of the breadth of his shoulders and forehead. He is also said to have been an expert wrestler and to have taken part in several important battles.

He was the devoted friend and pupil of Socrates, and during the imprisonment of his master he attended him constantly, and committed to writing his last discourses on the immortality of the soul.

After the death of Socrates it is supposed that Plato took refuge with Euclides in Megara, and subsequently extended his travels into Magna Graecia and Egypt.

Upon his return to Athens he taught those who came to him for instruction in the grove named Academus, near the Cephisus, and thus founded the first great philosophical school, over which he continued to preside until the day of his death. Above the entrance to this grove was inscribed the legend: "Let no one ignorant of geometry enter here." Here he was attended by persons of every description, among the more illustrious of whom were Aristotle, Lycurgus, Demosthenes and Isocrates.

There is a story to the effect that Plato three times visited Sicily, once upon the invitation of the elder Dionysius, and twice at the earnest solicitations of the younger. The former he is said to have so seriously offended as to cause the tyrant to have him seized on his return home and sold as a slave, from which state of bondage he was, however, released by Anicerius of Cyrene.

The people of his time thought more of him than they did of all their other philosophers, and called him the Divine Plato. So great was the regard and veneration for him that it was considered better to err with Plato than be right with anyone else.

The writings of Plato are numerous, and most of them are in the form of dialogues. The following pages contain translations of three of his works, viz.: "The Apologia," "The Crito" and "The Phædo," all of which have reference to the trial, imprisonment and death of Socrates.

"The Apologia" represents Socrates on trial for his life, undertaking his own defense, though unaccustomed to the language of the courts, the occasion being, as he says, the first time he has ever been before a court of justice, though seventy years of age. Plato was present at the trial, and no doubt gives us the very arguments used by the accused. Two charges were brought against Socrates— one that he did not believe in the gods recognized by the State, the other that he had corrupted the Athenian youth by his teachings. Socrates does not have recourse to the ordinary methods adopted by orators on similar occasions. He prefers to stand upon his own integrity and innocence, uninfluenced by the fear of that imaginary evil, death. He, therefore, does not firmly grapple with either of the charges preferred against him. He neither denies nor confesses the first accusation, but shows that in several instances he conformed to the religious customs of his country, and that he believes in God more than he fears man. The second charge he meets by a cross-examination of his accuser, Melitus, whom he reduces to the dilemma of charging him with corrupting the youth designedly, which would be absurd, or with doing so undesignedly, for which he could not be liable to punishment.

His defense, however, avails him nothing, and he is condemned by the judges to die by drinking the poisonous hemlock. In the closing part of "The Apologia" Socrates is represented as commenting upon the sentence which has been passed upon him, and as expressing his belief that in going to his death he is only passing to a better and a happier life.

In "The Crito" Socrates is represented in conversation with a friend of his named Crito, who had been present at his trial, and who had offered to assist Socrates in paying a fine, had a fine been the sentence imposed. Crito visits Socrates in his confinement to bring to him the intelligence that the ship, the arrival of which was to be the signal for his death upon the following day, would arrive forthwith, and to urge him to adopt the means of escape which had already been prepared. Socrates promises to follow the advice of Crito if, upon a full discussion of the matter, it seems right to do so. In the conversation which ensues Socrates argues that it is wrong to return evil for evil and that the obligations which a citizen owes to his State are more binding than those which a child owes his parents or a slave his master, and, therefore, it is his duty to submit to the laws of Athens at whatever cost to himself. Crito has no answer to make to this argument, and Socrates thereupon decides to submit to his fate.

Plato is said to have had two objects in writing this dialogue: First, to acquit Socrates of the charge of corrupting the Athenian youth; and, second, to establish the fact that it is necessary under all circumstances to submit to the established laws of his country.

"The Phædo" relates the manner in which Socrates spent the last day of his life and the circumstances attending his death. He is visited by a number of his friends, among whom are Phædo, Simmias and Crito. When his friends arrive they find him sitting upon a bed rubbing his legs, which have just been released from bonds. He remarks upon the unaccountable connection between pleasure and pain, and from this the conversation gradually turns to a consideration of the question of the immortality of the soul. He convinces his listeners of the pre-existence of the soul; but they are still skeptical as to its immortality, urging that its pre-existence and the fact that it is more durable than the body does not preclude the possibility of its being mortal. Socrates, however, argues that contraries cannot exist in the same thing at the same time, as, for example, the same object cannot partake of both magnitude and littleness at the same time. In like manner, heat while it is heat can never admit the idea of cold. Life and death are contraries and can never coexist; but wherever there is life there is soul, so that the soul contains that which is contrary to death and can never admit death; consequently the soul is immortal.

Having convinced his listeners, Socrates bathes and takes leave of his children and the women of his family. Thereupon the officer appears and tells him it is time for him to drink the poison. At this his friends commence to weep and are rebuked by Socrates for their weakness. He drinks the poison calmly and without hesitation, and then begins to walk about, still conversing with his friends. His limbs soon grow stiff and heavy and he lays himself down upon his back. His last words are: "Crito, we owe a cock to Æsculapius; pay it, therefore, and do not neglect it."

The Apology of Socrates

I know not, O Athenians! how far you have been influenced by my accusers for my part, in listening to them I almost forgot myself, so plausible were their arguments however, so to speak, they have said nothing true. But of the many falsehoods which they uttered I wondered at one of them especially, that in which they said that you ought to be on your guard lest you should be deceived by me, as being eloquent in speech. For that they are not ashamed of being forthwith convicted by me in fact, when I shall show that I am not by any means eloquent, this seemed to me the most shameless thing in them, unless indeed they call him eloquent who speaks the truth. For, if they mean this, then I would allow that I am an orator, but not after their fashion for they, as I affirm, have said nothing true, but from me you shall hear the whole truth. Not indeed, Athenians, arguments highly wrought, as theirs were, with choice phrases and expressions, nor adorned, but you shall hear a speech uttered without premeditation in such words as first present themselves. For I am confident that what I say will be just, and let none of you expect otherwise, for surely it would not become my time of life to come before you like a youth with a got up speech. Above all things, therefore, I beg and implore this of you, O Athenians! if you hear me defending myself in the same language as that in which I am accustomed to speak both in the forum at the counters, where many of you have heard me, and elsewhere, not to be surprised or disturbed on this account. For the case is this: I now for the first time come before a court of justice, though more than seventy years old; I am therefore utterly a stranger to the language here. As, then, if I were really a stranger, you would have pardoned me if I spoke in the language and the manner in which I had been educated, so now I ask this of you as an act of justice, as it appears to me, to disregard the manner of my speech, for perhaps it may be somewhat worse, and perhaps better, and to consider this only, and to give your attention to this, whether I speak what is just or not; for this is the virtue of a judge, but of an orator to speak the truth.

First, then, O Athenians! I am right in defending myself against the first false accusations alleged against me, and my first accusers, and then against the latest accusations, and the latest accusers. For many have been accusers of me to you, and for many years, who have asserted nothing true, of whom I am more afraid than of Anytus and his party, although they too are formidable; but those are still more formidable, Athenians, who, laying hold of many of you from childhood, have persuaded you, and accused me of what is not true: "that there is one Socrates, a wise man, who occupies himself about celestial matters, and has explored everything under the earth, and makes the worse appear the better reason." Those, O Athenians! who have spread abroad this report are my formidable accusers; for they who hear them think that such as search into these things do not believe that there are gods. In the next place, these accusers are numerous, and have accused me now for a long time; moreover, they said these things to you at that time of life in which you were most credulous, when you were boys and some of you youths, and they accused me altogether in my absence, when there was no one to defend me. But the most unreasonable thing of all is, that it is not possible to learn and mention their names, except that one of them happens to be a comic poet.[1] Such, however, as, influenced by envy and calumny, have persuaded you, and those who, being themselves persuaded, have persuaded others, all these are most difficult to deal with; for it is not possible to bring any of them forward here, nor to confute any; but it is altogether necessary to fight, as it were with a shadow, in making my defense, and to convict when there is no one to answer. Consider, therefore, as I have said, that my accusers are twofold, some who have lately accused me, and others long since, whom I have made mention of; and believe that I ought to defend myself against these first; for you heard them accusing me first, and much more than these last.

Well. I must make my defense, then, O Athenians! and endeavor in this so short a space of time to remove from your minds the calumny which you have long entertained. I wish, indeed, it might be so, if it were at all better both for you and me, and that in making my defense I could affect something more advantageous still: I think, however, that it will be difficult, and I am not entirely ignorant what the difficulty is. Nevertheless, let this turn out as may be pleasing to God, I must obey the law and make my defense.

Let us, then, repeat from the beginning what the accusation is from which the calumny against me has arisen, and relying on which Melitus has preferred this indictment against me. Well. What, then, do they who charge me say in their charge? For it is necessary to read their deposition as of public accusers. "Socrates acts wickedly, and is criminally curious in searching into things under the earth, and in the heavens, and in making the worse appear the better cause, and in teaching these same things to others." Such is the accusation: for such things you have yourselves seen in the comedy of Aristophanes, one Socrates there carried about, saying that he walks in the air, and acting many other buffooneries, of which I understand nothing whatever. Nor do I say this as disparaging such a science, if there be anyone skilled in such things, only let me not be prosecuted by Melitus on a charge of this kind; but I say it, O Athenians!

because I have nothing to do with such matters. And I call upon most of you as witnesses of this, and require you to inform and tell each other, as many of you as have ever heard me conversing; and there are many such among you. Therefore tell each other, if anyone of you has ever heard me conversing little or much on such subjects. And from this you will know that other things also, which the multitude assert of me, are of a similar nature.

However not one of these things is true; nor, if you have heard from anyone that I attempt to teach men, and require payment, is this true. Though this, indeed, appears to me to be an honorable thing, if one should be able to instruct men, like Gorgias the Leontine, Prodicus the Cean, and Hippias the Elean. For each of these, O Athenians! is able, by going through the several cities, to persuade the young men, who can attach themselves gratuitously to such of their own fellow-citizens as they please, to abandon their fellow-citizens and associate with them, giving them money and thanks besides. There is also another wise man here, a Parian, who, I hear, is staying in the city. For I happened to visit a person who spends more money on the sophists than all others together: I mean Callias, son of Hipponicus. I therefore asked him, for he has two sons, "Callias," I said, "if your two sons were colts or calves, we should have had to choose a master for them, and hire a person who would make them excel in such qualities as belong to their nature; and he would have been a groom or an agricultural laborer. But now, since your sons are men, what master do you intend to choose for them? Who is there skilled in the qualities that become a man and a citizen? For I suppose you must have considered this, since you have sons. Is there anyone," I said, "or not?" "Certainly," he answered. "Who is he?" said I, "and whence does he come? and on what terms does he teach?" He replied, "Evenus the Parian, Socrates, for five minae." And I deemed Evenus happy, if he really possesses this art, and teaches admirably. And I too should think highly of myself, and be very proud, if I possessed this knowledge, but I possess it not, O Athenians.

Perhaps, one of you may now object: "But, Socrates, what have you done, then? Whence have these calumnies against you arisen? For surely if you had not busied yourself more than others, such a report and story would never have got abroad, unless you had done something different from what most men do. Tell us, therefore, what it is, that we may not pass a hasty judgment on you." He who speaks thus appears to me to speak justly, and I will endeavor to show you what it is that has occasioned me this character and imputation. Listen, then: to some of you perhaps I shall appear to jest, yet be assured that I shall tell you the whole truth. For I, O Athenians! have acquired this character through nothing else than a certain wisdom. Of what kind, then, is this wisdom? Perhaps it is merely human wisdom. For in this, in truth, I appear to be wise. They probably, whom I have just now mentioned, possessed a wisdom more than human, otherwise I know not what to say about it; for I am not acquainted with it, and whosoever says I am, speaks falsely, and for the purpose of calumniating me. But, O Athenians! do not cry out against me, even though I should seem to you to speak somewhat arrogantly. For the account which I am going to give you is not my own; but I shall refer to an authority whom you will deem worthy of credit. For I shall adduce to you the god at Delphi as a witness of my wisdom, if I have any, and of what it is. You doubtless know Chaerepho: he was my associate from youth, and the associate of most of you; he accompanied you in your late exile, and returned with you. You know, then, what kind of a man Chaerepho was, how earnest in whatever he undertook. Having once gone to Delphi, he ventured to make the following inquiry of the oracle (and, as I said, O Athenians! do not cry out), for he asked if there was anyone wiser than I. The Pythian thereupon answered that there was not one wiser; and of this, his brother here will give you proofs, since he himself is dead.

Consider, then, why I mention these things: it is because I am going to show you whence the calumny against me arose. For when I heard this, I reasoned thus with myself, What does the god mean? What enigma is this? For I am not conscious to myself that I am wise, either much or little. What, then, does he mean by saying that I am the wisest? For assuredly he does not speak falsely: that he could not do. And for a long time I was in doubt what he meant; afterward, with considerable difficulty, I had recourse to the following method of searching out his meaning. I went to one of those who have the character of being wise, thinking that there, if anywhere, I should confute the oracle, and show in answer to the response that This man is wiser than I, though you affirmed that I was the wisest. Having, then, examined this man (for there is no occasion to mention his name; he was, however, one of our great politicians, in examining whom I felt as I proceed to describe, O Athenians!), having fallen into conversation with him, this man appeared to be wise in the opinion of most other men, and especially in his own opinion, though in fact he was not so. I thereupon endeavored to show him that he fancied himself to be wise, but really was not. Hence I became odious, both to him and to many others who were present. When I left him, I reasoned thus with myself: I am wiser than this man, for neither of us appears to know anything great and good; but he fancies he knows something, although he knows nothing; whereas I, as I do not know anything, so I do not fancy I do. In this trifling particular, then, I appear to be wiser than he, because I do not fancy I know what I do not know. After that I went to another who was thought to be wiser than the former, and formed the very same opinion. Hence I became odious to him and to many others.

7. After this I went to others in turn, perceiving indeed, and grieving and alarmed, that I was making myself odious; however, it appeared necessary to regard the oracle of the god as of the greatest moment, and that, in order to discover its meaning, I must go to all who had the reputation of possessing any knowledge. And by the dog, O Athenians! for I must tell you the truth, I came to some such conclusion as this: those who bore the highest reputation appeared to me to be most deficient, in my researches in obedience to the god, and others who were considered inferior more nearly approaching to the possession of understanding. But I must relate to you my wandering, and the labors which I underwent, in order that the oracle might prove incontrovertible. For after the politicians I went to the poets, as well the tragic as the dithyrambic and others, expecting that here I should in very fact find myself more ignorant than they. Taking up, therefore, some of their poems, which appeared to me most elaborately finished, I questioned them as to their meaning, that at the same time I might learn something from them. I am ashamed, O Athenians! to tell you the truth; however, it must be told. For, in a word, almost all who were present could have given a better account of them than those by whom they had been composed. I soon discovered this, therefore, with regard to the poets, that they do not affect their object by wisdom, but by a certain natural inspiration, and under the influence of enthusiasm, like prophets and seers; for these also say many fine things, but they understand nothing that they say. The poets appeared to me to be affected in a similar manner; and at the same time I perceived that they considered themselves, on account of their poetry, to be the wisest of men in other things, in which they were not. I left them, therefore, under the persuasion that I was superior to them, in the same way that I was to the politicians.

At last, therefore, I went to the artisans. For I was conscious to myself that I knew scarcely anything, but I was sure that I should find them possessed of much beautiful knowledge. And in this I was not deceived; for they knew things which I did not, and in this respect they were wiser than I. But, O Athenians! even the best workmen appeared to me to have fallen into the same error as the poets; for each, because he excelled in the practice of his art, thought that he was very wise in other most important matters, and this mistake of theirs obscured the wisdom that they really possessed. I therefore asked myself, in behalf of the oracle, whether I should prefer to continue as I am, possessing none, either of their wisdom or their ignorance, or to have both as they have. I answered, therefore, to myself and to the oracle, that it was better for me to continue as I am.

From this investigation, then, O Athenians! many enmities have arisen against me, and those the most grievous and severe, so that many calumnies have sprung from them, and among them this appellation of being wise; for those who are from time to time present think that I am wise in those things, with respect to which I expose the ignorance of others. The god, however, O Athenians! appears to be really wise, and to mean this by his oracle: that human wisdom is worth little or nothing; and it is clear that he did not say this to Socrates, but made use of my name, putting me forward as an example, as if he had said, that man is the wisest among you, who, like Socrates, knows that he is in reality worth nothing with respect to wisdom. Still, therefore, I go about and search and inquire into these things, in obedience to the god, both among citizens and strangers, if I think anyone of them is wise; and when he appears to me not to be so, I take the part of the god, and show that he is not wise. And, in consequence of this occupation, I have no leisure to attend in any considerable degree to the affairs of the state or my own; but I am in the greatest poverty through my devotion to the service of the god.

In addition to this, young men, who have much leisure and belong to the wealthiest families, following me of their own accord, take great delight in hearing men put to the test, and often imitate me, and themselves attempt to put others to the test; and then, I think, they find a great abundance of men who fancy they know something, although they know little or nothing. Hence those who are put to the test by them are angry with me, and not with them, and say that "there is one Socrates, a most pestilent fellow, who corrupts the youth." And when anyone asks them by doing or teaching what, they have nothing to say, for they do not know; but, that they may not seem to be at a loss, they say such things as are ready at hand against all philosophers; "that he searches into things in heaven and things under the earth, that he does not believe there are gods, and that he makes the worse appear the better reason." For they would not, I think, be willing to tell the truth that they have been detected in pretending to possess knowledge, whereas they know nothing. Therefore, I think, being ambitions and vehement and numerous, and speaking systematically and persuasively about me, they have filled your ears, for a long time and diligently calumniating me. From among these, Melitus, Anytus and Lycon have attacked me; Melitus being angry on account of the poets, Anytus on account of the artisans and politicians, and Lycon on account of the rhetoricians. So that, as I said in the beginning, I should wonder if I were able in so short a time to remove from your minds a calumny that has prevailed so long. This, O Athenians! is the truth; and I speak it without concealing or disguising anything from you, much or little; though I very well know that by so doing I shall expose myself to odium. This, however, is a proof that I speak the truth, and that this is the nature of the calumny against me, and that these are its causes. And if you will investigate the matter, either now or hereafter, you will find it to be so.

With respect, then, to the charges which my first accusers have alleged against me, let this be a sufficient apology to you. To Melitus, that good and patriotic man, as he says, and to my later accusers, I will next endeavor to give an answer; and here, again, as there are different accusers, let us take up their deposition. It is pretty much as follows: "Socrates," it says, "acts unjustly in corrupting the youth, and in not believing in those gods in whom the city believes, but in other strange divinities." Such is the accusation; let us examine each particular of it. It says that I act unjustly in corrupting the youth. But I, O Athenians! say that Melitus acts unjustly, because he jests on serious subjects, rashly putting men upon trial, under pretense of being zealous and solicitous about things in which he never at any time took any concern. But that this is the case I will endeavor to prove to you.

Come, then, Melitus, tell me, do you not consider it of the greatest importance that the youth should be made as virtuous as possible?

Mel. I do.

Socr. Well, now, tell the judges who it is that makes them better, for it is evident that you know, since it concerns you so much; for, having detected me in corrupting them, as you say, you have cited me here, and accused me: come, then, say, and inform the judges who it is that makes them better. Do you see, Melitus, that you are silent, and have nothing to say? But does it not appear to you to be disgraceful, and a sufficient proof of what I say, that you never took any concern about the matter? But tell me, friend, who makes them better?

Mel. The laws.

Socr. I do not ask this, most excellent sir, but what man, who surely must first know this very thing, the laws?

Mel. These, Socrates, the judges.

Socr. How say you, Melitus? Are these able to instruct the youth, and make them better?

Mel. Certainly.

Socr. Whether all, or some of them, and others not?

Mel. All.

Socr. You say well, by Juno! and have found a great abundance of those that confer benefit. But what further? Can these hearers make them better, or not?

Mel. They, too, can.

Socr. And what of the senators?

Mel. The senators, also.

Socr. But, Melitus, do those who attend the public assemblies corrupt the younger men? or do they all make them better?

Mel. They too.

Socr. All the Athenians, therefore, as it seems, make them honorable and good, except me; but I alone corrupt them. Do you say so?

Mel. I do assert this very thing.

Socr. You charge me with great ill-fortune. But answer me: does it appear to you to be the same, with respect to horses? Do all men make them better, and is there only someone that spoils them? or does quite the contrary of this take place? Is there someone person who can make them better, or very few; that is, the trainers? But if the generality of men should meddle with and make use of horses, do they spoil them? Is not this the case, Melitus, both with respect to horses and all other animals? It certainly is so, whether you and Anytus deny it or not. For it would be a great good-fortune for the youth if only one person corrupted, and the rest benefited them. However, Melitus, you have sufficiently shown that you never bestowed any care upon youth; and you clearly evince your own negligence, in that you have never paid any attention to the things with respect to which you accuse me.

Tell us further, Melitus, in the name of Jupiter, whether is it better to dwell with good or bad citizens? Answer, my friend; for I ask you nothing difficult. Do not the bad work some evil to those that are continually near them, but the good some good?

Mel. Certainly.

Socr. Is there anyone that wishes to be injured rather than benefited by his associates? Answer, good man; for the law requires you to answer. Is there anyone who wishes to be injured?

Mel. No, surely.

Socr. Come, then, whether do you accuse me here, as one that corrupts the youth, and makes them more depraved, designedly or undesignedly?

Mel. Designedly, I say.

Socr. What, then, Melitus, are you at your time of life so much wiser than I at my time of life, as to know that the evil are always working some evil to those that are most near to them, and the good some good; but I have arrived at such a pitch of ignorance as not to know that if I make anyone of my associates depraved, I shall be in danger of receiving some evil from him; and yet I designedly bring about this so great evil, as you say? In this I cannot believe you, Melitus, nor do I think would any other man in the world. But either I do not corrupt the youth, or, if I do corrupt them, I do it undesignedly: so that in both cases you speak falsely. But if I corrupt them undesignedly, for such involuntary offenses it is not usual to accuse one here, but to take one apart, and teach and admonish one. For it is evident that if I am taught, I shall cease doing what I do undesignedly. But you shunned me, and were not willing to associate with and instruct me; but you accuse me here, where it is usual to accuse those who need punishment, and not instruction.

Thus, then, O Athenians! this now is clear that I have said; that Melitus never paid any attention to these matters, much or little. However, tell us, Melitus, how you say I corrupt the youth? Is it not evidently, according to the indictment which you have preferred, by teaching them not to believe in the gods in whom the city believes, but in other strange deities? Do you not say that, by teaching these things, I corrupt the youth?

Mel. Certainly I do say so.

Socr. By those very gods, therefore, Melitus, of whom the discussion now is, speak still more clearly both to me and to these men. For I cannot understand whether you say that I teach them to believe that there are certain gods (and in that case I do believe that there are gods, and am not altogether an atheist, nor in this respect to blame), not, however, those which the city believes in, but others; and this it is that you accuse me of, that I introduce others. Or do you say outright that I do not myself believe that there are gods, and that I teach others the same?

Mel. I say this: that you do not believe in any gods at all.

Socr. O wonderful Melitus, how come you to say this? Do I not, then, like the rest of mankind, believe that the sun and moon are gods?

Mel. No, by Jupiter, O judges! for he says that the sun is a stone, and the moon an earth.

Socr. You fancy that you are accusing Anaxagoras, my dear Melitus, and thus you put a slight on these men, and suppose them to be so illiterate as not to know that the books of Anaxagoras of Clazomene are full of such assertions. And the young, moreover, learn these things from me, which they might purchase for a drachma, at most, in the orchestra, and so ridicule Socrates, if he pretended they were his own, especially since they are so absurd? I ask then, by Jupiter, do I appear to you to believe that there is no god?

Mel. No, by Jupiter, none whatever.

Socr. You say what is incredible, Melitus, and that, as appears to me, even to yourself. For this man, O Athenians! appears to me to be very insolent and intemperate and to have preferred this indictment through downright insolence, intemperance, and wantonness. For he seems, as it were, to have composed an enigma for the purpose of making an experiment. Whether will Socrates the wise know that I am jesting, and contradict myself, or shall I deceive him and all who hear me? For, in my opinion, he clearly contradicts himself in the indictment, as if he should say, Socrates is guilty of wrong in not believing that there are gods, and in believing that there are gods. And this, surely, is the act of one who is trifling.

Consider with me now, Athenians, in what respect he appears to me to say so. And do you, Melitus, answer me; and do ye, as I besought you at the outset, remember not to make an uproar if I speak after my usual manner.

Is there any man, Melitus, who believes that there are human affairs, but does not believe that there are men? Let him answer, judges, and not make so much

15

noise. Is there anyone who does not believe that there are horses, but that there are things pertaining to horses? or who does not believe that there are pipers, but that there are things pertaining to pipes? There is not, O best of men! for since you are not willing to answer, I say it to you and to all here present. But answer to this at least: is there anyone who believes that there are things relating to demons, but does not believe that there are demons?

Mel. There is not.

Socr. How obliging you are in having hardly answered; though compelled by these judges! You assert, then, that I do believe and teach things relating to demons, whether they be new or old; therefore, according to your admission, I do believe in things relating to demons, and this you have sworn in the bill of indictment. If, then, I believe in things relating to demons, there is surely an absolute necessity that I should believe that there are demons. Is it not so? It is. For I suppose you to assent, since you do not answer. But with respect to demons, do we not allow that they are gods, or the children of gods? Do you admit this or not?

Mel. Certainly.

Socr. Since, then, I allow that there are demons, as you admit, if demons are a kind of gods, this is the point in which I say you speak enigmatically and divert yourself in saying that I do not allow there are gods, and again that I do allow there are, since I allow that there are demons? But if demons are the children of gods, spurious ones, either from nymphs or any others, of whom they are reported to be, what man can think that there are sons of gods, and yet that there are not gods? For it would be just as absurd as if anyone should think that there are mules, the offspring of horses and asses, but should not think there are horses and asses. However, Melitus, it cannot be otherwise than that you have preferred this indictment for the purpose of trying me, or because you were at a loss what real crime to allege against me; for that you should persuade any man who has the smallest degree of sense that the same person can think that there are things relating to demons and to gods, and yet that there are neither demons, nor gods, not heroes, is utterly impossible.

That I am not guilty, then, O Athenians! according to the indictment of Melitus, appears to me not to require a lengthened defense; but what I have said is sufficient. And as to what I said at the beginning, that there is a great enmity toward me among the multitude, be assured it is true. And this it is which will condemn me, if I am condemned, not Melitus, nor Anytus, but the calumny and envy of the multitude, which have already condemned many others, and those good men, and will, I think, condemn others also; for there is no danger that it will stop with me.

Perhaps, however, someone may say, "Are you not ashamed, Socrates, to have pursued a study from which you are now in danger of dying?" To such a person I should answer with good reason, You do not say well, friend, if you think that a man, who is even of the least value, ought to take into the account the risk of life or death, and ought not to consider that alone when he performs any action, whether he is acting justly or unjustly, and the part of a good man or bad man. For, according to your reasoning, all those demi-gods that died at Troy would be vile characters, as well all the rest as the son of Thetis, who so far despised danger in comparison of submitting to disgrace, that when his mother, who was a goddess, spoke to him, in his impatience to kill Hector, something to this effect, as I think,[2] "My son, if you revenge the death of your friend Patroclus, and slay Hector, you will yourself die, for," she said, "death awaits you immediately after Hector;" but he, on hearing this, despised death and danger, and dreading much more to live as a coward, and not avenge his friend, said, "May I die immediately when I have inflicted punishment on the guilty, that I may not stay here an object of ridicule, by the curved ships, a burden to the ground?"—do you think that he cared for death and danger? For thus it is, O Athenians! in truth: wherever anyone has posted himself, either thinking it to be better, or has been posted by his chief, there, as it appears to me, he ought to remain and meet danger, taking no account either of death or anything else in comparison with disgrace.

I then should be acting strangely, O Athenians! if, when the generals whom you chose to command me assigned me my post at Potidæ, at Amphipolis, and at Delium, I then remained where they posted me, like any other person, and encountered the danger of death; but when the deity, as I thought and believed, assigned it as my duty to pass my life in the study of philosophy, and examining myself and others, I should on that occasion, through fear of death or anything else whatsoever, desert my post, strange indeed would it be; and then, in truth, anyone might justly bring me to trial, and accuse me of not believing in the gods, from disobeying the oracle, fearing death, and thinking myself to be wise when I am not. For to fear death, O Athenians! is nothing else than to appear to be wise, without being so; for it is to appear to know what one does not know. For no one knows but that death is the greatest of all good to man; but men fear it, as if they well knew that it is the greatest of evils. And how is not this the most reprehensible ignorance, to think that one knows what one does not know? But I, O Athenians! in this, perhaps, differ from most men; and if I should say that I am in anything wiser than another, it would be in this, that not having a competent knowledge of the things in Hades, I also think that I have not such knowledge. But to act unjustly, and to disobey my superior, whether God or man, I know is evil and base. I shall never, therefore, fear or shun things which, for aught I

17

know, maybe good, before evils which I know to be evils. So that, even if you should now dismiss me, not yielding to the instances of Anytus, who said that either I should not[3] appear here at all, or that, if I did appear, it was impossible not to put me to death, telling you that if I escaped, your sons, studying what Socrates teaches, would all be utterly corrupted; if you should address me thus, "Socrates, we shall not now yield to Anytus, but dismiss you, on this condition, however, that you no longer persevere in your researches nor study philosophy; and if hereafter you are detected in so doing, you shall die"—if, as I said, you should dismiss, me on these terms, I should say to you, "O Athenians! I honor and love you; but I shall obey God rather than you; and so long as I breathe and am able, I shall not cease studying philosophy, and exhorting you and warning anyone of you I may happen to meet, saying, as I have been accustomed to do: 'O best of men! seeing you are an Athenian, of a city the most powerful and most renowned for wisdom and strength, are you not ashamed of being careful for riches, how you may acquire them in greatest abundance, and for glory, and honor, but care not nor take any thought for wisdom and truth, and for your soul, how it may be made most perfect?'" And if anyone of you should question my assertion, and affirm that he does care for these things, I shall not at once let him go, nor depart, but I shall question him, sift and prove him. And if he should appear to me not to possess virtue, but to pretend that he does, I shall reproach him for that he sets the least value on things of the greatest worth, but the highest on things that are worthless. Thus I shall act to all whom I meet, both young and old, stranger and citizen, but rather to you, my fellow-citizens, because ye are more nearly allied to me. For be well assured, this the deity commands. And I think that no greater good has ever befallen you in the city than my zeal for the service of the god. For I go about doing nothing else than persuading you, both young and old, to take no care either for the body, or for riches, prior to or so much as for the soul, how it may be made most perfect, telling you that virtue does not spring from riches, but riches and all other human blessings, both private and public, from virtue. If, then, by saying these things, I corrupt the youth, these things must be mischievous; but if anyone says that I speak other things than these, he misleads you.[4] Therefore I must say, O Athenians! either yield to Anytus, or do not, either dismiss me or not, since I shall not act otherwise, even though I must die many deaths.

Murmur not, O Athenians! but continue to attend to my request, not to murmur at what I say, but to listen, for, as I think, you will derive benefit from listening. For I am going to say other things to you, at which, perhaps, you will raise a clamor; but on no account do so. Be well assured, then, if you put me to death, being such a man as I say I am, you will not injure me more than yourselves. For neither will Melitus nor Anytus harm me; nor have they the power; for I do not think that it is possible for a better man to be injured by a worse. He may perhaps have me condemned to death, or banished, or deprived of civil rights; and he or others may perhaps consider these as mighty evils; I, however, do not consider them so, but that it is much more so to do what he is now doing, to endeavor to put a man to death unjustly. Now, therefore, O Athenians! I am far from making a defense on my behalf, as anyone might think, but I do so on your own behalf, lest by condemning me you should offend at all with respect to the gift of the deity to you. For, if you should put me to death, you will not easily find such another, though it may be ridiculous to say so, altogether attached by the deity to this city as to a powerful and generous horse, somewhat sluggish from his size, and requiring to be roused by a gad-fly; so the deity appears to have united me, being such a person as I am, to the city, that I may rouse you, and persuade and reprove every one of you, nor ever cease besetting you throughout the whole day. Such another man, O Athenians! will not easily be found; therefore, if you will take my advice, you will spare me. But you, perhaps, being irritated like drowsy persons who are roused from sleep, will strike me, and, yielding to Anytus, will unthinkingly condemn me to death; and then you will pass the rest of your life in sleep, unless the deity, caring for you, should send someone else to you. But that I am a person who has been given by the deity to this city, you may discern from hence; for it is not like the ordinary conduct of men, that I should have neglected all my own affairs, and suffered my private interest to be neglected for so many years, and that I should constantly attend to your concerns, addressing myself to each of you separately, like a father, or elder brother, persuading you to the pursuit of virtue. And if I had derived any profit from this course, and had received pay for my exhortations, there would have been some reason for my conduct; but now you see yourselves that my accusers, who have so shamelessly calumniated me in everything else, have not had the impudence to charge me with this, and to bring witnesses to prove that I ever either exacted or demanded any reward. And I think I produce a sufficient proof that I speak the truth, namely, my poverty.

Perhaps, however, it may appear absurd that I, going about, thus advise you in private and make myself busy, but never venture to present myself in public before your assemblies and give advice to the city. The cause of this is that which you have often and in many places heard me mention; because I am moved by a certain divine and spiritual influence, which also Melitus, through mockery, has set out in the indictment. This began with me from childhood, being a kind of voice which, when present, always diverts me from what I am about to do, but never urges me on. This it is which opposed my meddling in public politics; and it appears to me to have opposed me very properly. For be well assured, O Athenians! if I had long since attempted to intermeddle with politics, I should have perished long ago, and should not have at all benefited you or myself. And be not angry with me for speaking the truth. For it is not possible that any man should be safe who sincerely opposes either you, or any other multitude, and who prevents many unjust and illegal actions from being committed in a city; but it is necessary that he who in earnest contends for justice, if he will be safe for but a short time, should live privately, and take no part in public affairs.

I will give you strong proofs of this, not words, but what you value, facts. Hear, then, what has happened to me, that you may know that I would not yield to anyone contrary to what is just, through fear of death, at the same time by not yielding I must perish. I shall tell you what will be displeasing and wearisome,[5] yet true. For I, O Athenians! never bore any other magisterial office in the city, but have been a senator: and our Antiochean tribe happened to supply the Prytanes when you chose to condemn in a body the ten generals who had not taken off those that perished in the sea-fight, in violation of the law, as you afterward all thought. At that time I alone of the Prytanes opposed your doing anything contrary to the laws, and I voted against you; and when the orators were ready to denounce me, and to carry me before a magistrate, and you urged and cheered them on, I thought I ought rather to meet the danger with law and justice on my side, than through fear of imprisonment or death, to take part with you in your unjust designs. And this happened while the city was governed by a democracy. But when it became an oligarchy, the Thirty, having sent for me with four others to the Tholus, ordered us to bring Leon the Salaminian from Salamis, that he might be put to death; and they gave many similar orders to many others, wishing to involve as many as they could in guilt. Then, however, I showed, not in word but indeed, that I did not care for death, if the expression be not too rude, in the smallest degree; but that all my care was to do nothing unjust or unholy. For that government, strong as it was, did not so overawe me as to make me commit an unjust action; but when we came out from the Tholus, the four went to Salamis, and brought back Leon; but I went away home. And perhaps for this I should have been put to death, if that government had not been speedily broken up. And of this you can have many witnesses.

Do you think, then, that I should have survived so many years if I had engaged in public affairs, and, acting as becomes a good man, had aided the cause of justice, and, as I ought, had deemed this of the highest importance? Far from it, O Athenians! nor would any other man have done so. But I, through the whole of my life, if I have done anything in public, shall be found to be a man, and the very same in private, who has never made a concession to anyone contrary to justice, neither to any other, nor to anyone of these whom my calumniators say are my disciples. I, however, was never the preceptor of anyone; but if anyone desired to hear me speaking, and to see me busied about my own mission, whether he were young or old, I never refused him. Nor do I discourse when I receive money, and not when I do not receive any, but I allow both rich and poor alike to question me, and, if anyone wishes it, to answer me and hear what I have to say. And for these, whether anyone proves to be a good man or not, I cannot justly be responsible, because I never either promised them any instruction or taught them at all. But if anyone says that he has ever learned or heard anything from me in private which all others have not, be well assured that he does not speak the truth.

But why do some delight to spend so long a time with me? Ye have heard, O Athenians! I have told you the whole truth, that they delight to hear those closely questioned who think that they are wise but are not; for this is by no means disagreeable. But this duty, as I say, has been enjoined me by the deity, by oracles, by dreams, and by every mode by which any other divine decree has ever enjoined anything to man to do. These things, O Athenians! are both true, and easily confuted if not true. For if I am now corrupting some of the youths, and have already corrupted others, it were fitting, surely, that if any of them, having become advanced in life, had discovered that I gave them bad advice when they were young, they should now rise up against me, accuse me, and have me punished; or if they were themselves unwilling to do this, some of their kindred, their fathers, or brothers, or other relatives, if their kinsman have ever sustained any damage from me, should now call it to mind. Many of them, however, are here present, whom I see: first, Crito, my contemporary and fellow-burgher, father of this Critobulus; then Lysanias of Sphettus, father of this ᴣschines; again, Antiphon of Cephisus, father of Epigenes. There are those others, too, whose brothers maintained the same intimacy with me, namely, Nicostratus, son of Theodotus, brother of Theodotus—Theodotus indeed is dead, so that he could not deprecate his brother's proceedings—and Paralus here, son of Demodocus, whose brother was Theages; and Adimantus, son of Ariston, whose brother is this Plato; and ᴣantodorus, whose brother is this Apollodorus. I could also mention many others to you, someone of whom certainly Melitus ought to have adduced in his speech as a witness. If, however, he then forgot to do so, let him now adduce them; I give him leave to do so, and let him say it, if he has anything of the kind to allege. But, quite contrary to this, you will find, O Athenians! all ready to assist me, who have corrupted and injured their relatives, as Melitus and Anytus say. For those who have been themselves corrupted might perhaps have some reason for assisting me; but those who have not been corrupted, men now advanced in life, their relatives, what other reason can they have for assisting me, except that right and just one, that they know that Melitus speaks falsely, and that I speak the truth.

23. Well, then, Athenians, these are pretty much the things I have to say in my defense, and others perhaps of the same kind. Perhaps, however, some among you will be indignant on recollecting his own case, if he, when engaged in a cause far less than this, implored and besought the judges with many tears, bringing forward his children in order that he might excite their utmost compassion, and many others of his relatives and friends, whereas I do none of these things, although I may appear to be incurring the extremity of danger. Perhaps, therefore, someone, taking notice of this, may become more determined against me, and, being enraged at this very conduct of mine, may give his vote under the influence of anger. If, then, anyone of you is thus affected—I do not, however, suppose that there is—but if there should be, I think I may reasonably say to him: "I, too, O best of men, have relatives; for, to make use of that saying of Homer, I am not sprung from an oak, nor from a rock, but from men, so that I, too, O Athenians! have relatives, and three sons, one now grown up, and two boys: I shall not, however, bring anyone of them forward and implore you to acquit me." Why, then, shall I not do this? Not from contumacy, O Athenians! nor disrespect toward you. Whether or not I am undaunted at the prospect of death is another question; but, out of regard to my own character, and yours, and that of the whole city, it does not appear to me to be honorable that I should do anything of this kind at my age, and with the reputation I have, whether true or false. For it is commonly agreed that Socrates in some respects excels the generality of men. If, then, those among you who appear to excel either in wisdom, or fortitude, or any other virtue whatsoever, should act in such a manner as I have often seen some when they have been brought to trial, it would be shameful, who appearing indeed to be something, have conducted themselves in a surprising manner, as thinking they should suffer something dreadful by dying, and as if they would be immortal if you did not put them to death. Such men appear to me to bring disgrace on the city, so that any stranger might suppose that such of the Athenians as excel in virtue, and whom they themselves choose in preference to themselves for magistracies and other honors, are in no respect superior to women. For these things, O Athenians! neither ought we to do who have attained to any height of reputation, nor, should we do them, ought you to suffer us; but you should make this manifest, that you will much rather condemn him who introduces these piteous dramas, and makes the city ridiculous, than him who quietly awaits your decision.

But, reputation apart, O Athenians! it does not appear to me to be right to entreat a judge, or to escape by entreaty; but one ought to inform and persuade him. For a judge does not sit for the purpose of administering justice out of favor, but that he may judge rightly, and he is sworn not to show favor to whom he pleases, but that he will decide according to the laws. It is, therefore, right that neither should we accustom you, nor should you accustom yourselves, to violate your oaths; for in so doing neither of us would act righteously. Think not then, O Athenians! that I ought to adopt such a course toward you as I neither consider honorable, nor just, nor holy, as well, by Jupiter! on any other occasion, and now especially when I am accused of impiety by this Melitus. For clearly, if I should persuade you, and by my entreaties should put a constraint on you who are bound by an oath, I should teach you to think that there are no gods, and in reality, while making my defense, should accuse myself of not believing in the gods. This, however, is far from being the case; for I believe, O Athenians! as none of my accusers do, and I leave it to you and to the deity to judge concerning me in such way as will be best both for me and for you.

[Socrates here concludes his defense, and, the votes being taken, he is declared guilty by a majority of voices. He thereupon resumes his address.]

That I should not be grieved, O Athenians! at what has happened—namely, that you have condemned me—as well many other circumstances concur in bringing to pass; and, moreover this, that what has happened has not happened contrary to my expectation; but I much rather wonder at the number of votes on either side. For I did not expect that I should be condemned by so small a number, but by a large majority; but now, as it seems, if only three more votes had changed sides, I should have been acquitted. So far as Melitus is concerned, as it appears to me, I have been already acquitted; and not only have I been acquitted, but it is clear to everyone that had not Anytus and Lycon come forward to accuse me, he would have been fined a thousand drachmas, for not having obtained a fifth part of the votes.

The man, then, awards me the penalty of death. Well. But what shall I, on my part, O Athenians! Award myself? Is it not clear that it will be such as I deserve? What, then, is that? Do I deserve to suffer, or to pay a fine? for that I have purposely during my life not remained quiet, but neglecting what most men seek after, money-making, domestic concerns, military command, popular oratory, and, moreover, all the magistracies, conspiracies, and cabals that are met with in the city, thinking that I was in reality too upright a man to be safe if I took part in such things, I therefore did not apply myself to those pursuits, by attending to which I should have been of no service either to you or to myself; but in order to confer the greatest benefit on each of you privately, as I affirm, I thereupon applied myself to that object, endeavoring to persuade every one of you not to take any care of his own affairs before he had taken care of himself in what way he may become the best and wisest, nor of the affairs of the city before he took care of the city itself; and that he should attend to other things in the same manner. What treatment, then, do I deserve, seeing I am such a man? Some reward, O Athenians! if, at least, I am to be estimated according to my real deserts; and, moreover, such a reward as would be suitable to me. What, then, is suitable to a poor man, a benefactor, and who has need of leisure in order to give you good advice? There is nothing so suitable, O Athenians! as that such a man should be maintained in the Prytaneum, and this much more than if one of you had been victorious at the Olympic games in a horserace, or in the two or four horsed chariot race: for such a one makes you appear to be happy, but I, to be so; and he does not need support, but I do. If, therefore, I must award a sentence according to my just deserts, I award this, maintenance in the Prytaneum.

Perhaps, however, in speaking to you thus, I appear to you to speak in the same presumptuous manner as I did respecting commiseration and entreaties; but such is not the case, O Athenians! it is rather this: I am persuaded that I never designedly injured any man, though I cannot persuade you of this, for we have conversed with each other but for a short time. For if there were the same law with you as with other men, that in capital cases the trial should list not only one day, but many, I think you would be persuaded; but it is not easy in a short time to do away with, great calumnies. Being persuaded, then, that I have injured no one, I am far from intending to injure myself, and of pronouncing against myself that I am deserving of punishment, and from awarding myself anything of the kind. Through fear of what? lest I should suffer that which Melitus awards me, of which I say I know not whether it be good or evil? Instead of this, shall I choose what I well know to be evil, and award that? Shall I choose imprisonment? And why should I live in prison, a slave to the established magistracy, the Eleven? Shall I choose a fine, and to be imprisoned until I have paid it? But this is the same as that which I just now mentioned, for I have not money to pay it. Shall I, then, award myself exile? For perhaps you would consent to this award. I should indeed be very fond of life, O Athenians! if I were so devoid of reason as not to be able to reflect that you, who are my fellow-citizens, have been unable to endure my manner of life and discourses, but they have become so burdensome and odious to you that you now seek to be rid of them: others, however, will easily bear them. Far from it, O Athenians! A fine life it would be for me at my age to go out wandering, and driven from city to city, and so to live. For I well know that, wherever I may go, the youth will listen to me when I speak, as they do here. And if I repulse them, they will themselves drive me out, persuading the elders; and if I do not repulse them, their fathers and kindred will banish me on their account.

Perhaps, however, someone will say, Can you not, Socrates, when you have gone from us, live a silent and quiet life? This is the most difficult thing of all to persuade some of you. For if I say that that would be to disobey the deity, and that, therefore, it is impossible for me to live quietly, you would not believe me, thinking I spoke ironically. If, on the other hand, I say that this is the greatest good to man, to discourse daily on virtue, and other things which you have heard me discussing, examining both myself and others, but that a life without investigation is not worth living for, still less would you believe me if I said this. Such, however, is the case, as I affirm, O Athenians! though it is not easy to persuade you. And at the same time I am not accustomed to think myself deserving of any ill. If, indeed, I were rich, I would amerce myself in such a sum as I should be able to pay; for then I should have suffered no harm, but now—for I cannot, unless you are willing to amerce me in such a sum as I am able to pay. But perhaps I could pay you a mina of silver: in that sum, then, I amerce myself. But Plato here, O Athenians! and Crito Critobulus, and Apollodorus bid me amerce myself in thirty minae, and they offer to be sureties. I amerce myself, then, to you in that sum; and they will be sufficient sureties for the money.

[The judges now proceeded to pass the sentence, and condemned Socrates to death; whereupon he continued:]

For the sake of no long space of time, O Athenians! you will incur the character and reproach at the hands of those who wish to defame the city, of having put that wise man, Socrates, to death. For those who wish to defame you will assert that I am wise, though I am not. If, then, you had waited for a short time, this would have happened of its own accord; for observe my age, that it is far advanced in life, and near death. But I say this not to you all, but to those only who have condemned me to die. And I say this, too, to the same persons. Perhaps you think, O Athenians! that I have been convicted through the want of arguments, by which I might have persuaded you, had I thought it right to do and say anything, so that I might escape punishment. Far otherwise: I have been convicted through want indeed, yet not of arguments, but of audacity and impudence, and of the inclination to say such things to you as would have been most agreeable for you to hear, had I lamented and bewailed and done and said many other things unworthy of me, as I affirm, but such as you are accustomed to hear from others. But neither did I then think that I ought, for the sake of avoiding danger, to do anything unworthy of a freeman, nor do I now repent of having so defended myself; but I should much rather choose to die, having so defended myself, than to live in that way. For neither in a trial nor in battle is it right that I or anyone else should employ every possible means whereby he may avoid death; for in battle it is frequently evident that a man might escape death by laying down his arms, and throwing himself on the mercy of his pursuers. And there are many other devices in every danger, by which to avoid death, if a man dares to do and say everything. But this is not difficult, O Athenians! to escape death; but it is much more difficult to avoid depravity, for it runs swifter than death. And now I, being slow and aged, am overtaken by the slower of the two; but my accusers, being strong and active, have been overtaken by the swifter, wickedness. And now I depart, condemned by you to death; but they condemned by truth, as guilty of iniquity and injustice: and I abide my sentence, and so do they. These things, perhaps, ought so to be, and I think that they are for the best.

In the next place, I desire to predict to you who have condemned me, what will be your fate; for I am now in that condition in which men most frequently prophesy—namely, when they are about to die. I say, then, to you, O Athenians! who have condemned me to death, that immediately after my death a punishment will overtake you, far more severe, by Jupiter! than that which you have inflicted on me. For you have done this, thinking you should be freed from the necessity of giving an account of your lives. The very contrary, however, as I affirm, will happen to you. Your accusers will be more numerous, whom I have now restrained, though you did not perceive it; and they will be more severe, inasmuch as they are younger, and you will be more indignant. For if you think that by putting men to death you will restrain anyone from upbraiding you because you do not live well, you are much mistaken; for this method of escape is neither possible nor honorable; but that other is most honorable and most easy, not to put a check upon others, but for a man to take heed to himself how he may be most perfect. Having predicted thus much to those of you who have condemned me, I take my leave of you.

But with you who have voted for my acquittal I would gladly hold converse on what has now taken place, while the magistrates are busy, and I am not yet carried to the place where I must die. Stay with me, then, so long, O Athenians! for nothing hinders our conversing with each other, while we are permitted to do so; for I wish to make known to you, as being my friends, the meaning of that which has just now befallen me. To me, then, O my judges! and in calling you judges I call you rightly—a strange thing has happened. For the wonted prophetic voice of my guardian deity on every former occasion, even in the most trifling affairs, opposed me if I was about to do anything wrong; but now that has befallen me which ye yourselves behold, and which anyone would think, and which is supposed to be the extremity of evil; yet neither when I departed from home in the morning did the warning of the god oppose me, nor when I came up here to the place of trial, nor in my address when I was about to say anything; yet on other occasions it has frequently restrained me in the midst of speaking. But now it has never, throughout this proceeding, opposed me, either in what I did or said. What, then, do I suppose to be the cause of this? I will tell you: what has befallen me appears to be a blessing; and it is impossible that we think rightly who suppose that death is an evil. A great proof of this to me is the fact that it is impossible but that the accustomed signal should have opposed me, unless I had been about to meet with some good.

Moreover, we may hence conclude that there is great hope that death is a blessing. For to die is one of two things: for either the dead may be annihilated, and have no sensation of anything whatever; or, as it is said, there are a certain change and passage of the soul from one place to another. And if it is a privation of all sensation, as it were a sleep in which the sleeper has no dream, death would be a wonderful gain. For I think that if anyone, having selected a night in which he slept so soundly as not to have had a dream, and having compared this night with all the other nights and days of his life, should be required, on consideration, to say how many days and nights he had passed better and more pleasantly than this night throughout his life, I think that not only a private person, but even the great king himself, would find them easy to number, in comparison with other days and nights. If, therefore, death is a thing of this kind, I say it is a gain; for thus all futurity appears to be nothing more than one night. But if, on the other hand, death is a removal from hence to another place, and what is said be true, that all the dead are there, what greater blessing can there be than this, my judges? For if, on arriving at Hades, released from these who pretend to be judges, one shall find those who are true judges, and who are said to judge there, Minos and Rhadamanthus, Zacus and Triptolemus, and such others of the demi-gods as were just during their own life, would this be a sad removal? At what price would you not estimate a conference with Orpheus and Musaeus, Hesiod and Homer? I indeed should be willing to die often, if this be true. For to me the sojourn there would be admirable, when I should meet with Palamedes, and Ajax, son of Telamon, and any other of the ancients who has died by an unjust sentence. The comparing my sufferings with theirs would, I think, be no unpleasing occupation. But the greatest pleasure would be to spend my time in questioning and examining the people there as I have done those here, and discovering who among them is wise, and who fancies himself to be so, but is not. At what price, my judges, would not anyone estimate the opportunity of questioning him who led that mighty army against Troy, or Ulysses, or Sisyphus, or ten thousand others whom one might mention both men and women—with whom to converse and associate, and to question them, would be an inconceivable happiness? Surely for that the judges there do not condemn to death; for in other respects those who live there are more happy than those who are here, and are henceforth immortal, if, at least, what is said be true.

You, therefore, O my judges! ought to entertain good hopes with respect to death, and to meditate on this one truth, that to a good man nothing is evil, neither while living nor when dead, nor are his concerns neglected by the gods. And what has befallen me is not the effect of chance; but this is clear to me, that now to die, and be freed from my cares is better for me On this account the warning in no way turned me aside; and I bear no resentment toward those who condemned me, or against my accusers, although they did not condemn and accuse me with this intention, but thinking to injure me: in this they deserve to be blamed.

Thus much, however, I beg of them. Punish my sons when they grow up, O judges! paining them as I have pained you, if they appear to you to care for riches or anything else before virtue; and if they think themselves to be something when they are nothing, reproach them as I have done you, for not attending to what they ought, and for conceiving themselves to be something when they are worth nothing. If ye do this, both I and my sons shall have met with just treatment at your hands.

But it is now time to depart—for me to die, for you to live. But which of us is going to a better state is unknown to everyone but God.

Footnotes

[1] Aristophanes.

[2] "Iliad," lib. xviii. ver. 94, etc.

[3] See the "Crito," sec. 5.

[4] ouden legei, literally, "he says nothing:" on se trompe, ou l'on vous impose, Cousin.

[5] But for the authority of Stallbaum, I should have translated dikanika "forensic;" that is, such arguments as an advocate would use   in a court of justice.

Introduction to the Crito

It has been remarked by Stallbaum that Plato had a twofold design in this dialogue—one, and that the primary one, to free Socrates from the imputation of having attempted to corrupt the Athenian youth; the other, to establish the principle that under all circumstances it is the duty of a good citizen to obey the laws of his country. These two points, however, are so closely interwoven with each other, that the general principle appears only to be illustrated by the example of Socrates.

Crito was one of those friends of Socrates who had been present at his trial, and had offered to assist in paying a fine, had a fine been imposed instead of the sentence of death. He appears to have frequently visited his friend in prison after his condemnation; and now, having obtained access to his cell very early in the morning, finds him composed in a quiet sleep. He brings intelligence that the ship, the arrival of which would be the signal for his death on the following day, is expected to arrive forthwith, and takes occasion to entreat Socrates to make his escape, the means of which were already prepared. Socrates thereupon, having promised to follow the advice of Crito if, after the matter had been fully discussed, it should appear to be right to do so, proposes to consider the duty of a citizen toward his country; and having established the divine principle that it is wrong to return evil for evil, goes on to show that the obligations of a citizen to his country are even more binding than those of a child to its parent, or a slave to his master, and that therefore it is his duty to obey the established laws, at whatever cost to himself.

At length Crito admits that he has no answer to make, and Socrates resolves to submit himself to the will of Providence.

Crito; Or, the Duty of a Citizen

SOCRATES, CRITO.

Socr. Why have you come at this hour, Crito? Is it not very early?

Cri. It is.

Socr. About what time?

Cri. Scarce day-break.

Socr. I wonder how the keeper of the prison came to admit you.

Cri. He is familiar with me, Socrates, from my having frequently come hither; and he is under some obligations to me.

Socr. Have you just now come, or some time since?

Cri. A considerable time since.

Socr. Why, then, did you not wake me at once, instead of sitting down by me in silence?

Cri. By Jupiter! Socrates, I should not myself like to be so long awake, and in such affliction. But I have been for some time wondering at you, perceiving how sweetly you slept; and I purposely did not awake you, that you might pass your time as pleasantly as possible. And, indeed, I have often before throughout your whole life considered you happy in your disposition, but far more so in the present calamity, seeing how easily and meekly you bear it.

Socr. However, Crito, it would be disconsonant for a man at my time of life to repine because he must needs die.

Cri. But others, Socrates, at your age have been involved in similar calamities, yet their age has not hindered their repining at their present fortune.

Socr. So it is. But why did you come so early?

Cri. Bringing sad tidings, Socrates, not sad to you, as it appears, but to me, and all your friends, sad and heavy, and which I, I think, shall bear worst of all.

Socr. What tidings? Has the ship[6] arrived from Delos, on the arrival of which I must die?

Cri. It has not yet arrived, but it appears to me that it will come to-day, from what certain persons report who have come from Sunium,[7] and left it there. It is clear, therefore, from these messengers, that it will come to day, and consequently it will be necessary, Socrates, for you to die to-morrow.

30

2. Socr. But with good fortune, Crito, and if so it please the gods, so be it. I do not think, however, that it will come to day.

Cri. Whence do you form this conjecture?

Socr. I will tell you. I must die on the day after that on which the ship arrives.

Cri. So they say[8] who have the control of these things.

Socr. I do not think, then, that it will come to-day, but to-morrow. I conjecture this from a dream which I had this very night, not long ago, and you seem very opportunely to have refrained from waking me.

Cri. But what was this dream?

Socr. A beautiful and majestic woman, clad in white garments seemed to approach me, and to call to me and say, "Socrates, three days hence you will reach fertile Pythia"[9].

Cri. What a strange dream, Socrates!

Socr. Very clear, however, as it appears to me, Crito.

Cri. Very much so, as it seems. But, my dear Socrates, even now be persuaded by me, and save yourself. For if you die, not only a single calamity will befall me, but, besides being deprived of such a friend as I shall never meet with again, I shall also appear to many who do not know you and me well, when I might have saved you had I been willing to spend my money, to have neglected to do so. And what character can be more disgraceful than this—to appear to value one's riches more than one's friends? For the generality of men will not be persuaded that you were unwilling to depart hence, when we urged you to it.

Socr. But why, my dear Crito, should we care so much for the opinion of the many? For the most worthy men, whom we ought rather to regard, will think that matters have transpired as they really have.

Cri. Yet you see, Socrates, that it is necessary to attend to the opinion of the many. For the very circumstances of the present case show that the multitude are able to affect not only the smallest evils, but even the greatest, if anyone is calumniated to them.

Socr. Would, O Crito that the multitude could affect the greatest evils, that they might also effect the greatest good, for then it would be well. But now they can do neither; for they can make a man neither wise nor foolish; but they do whatever chances.

Cri. So let it be, then. But answer me this, Socrates: are you not anxious for me and other friends, lest, if you should escape from hence, informers should give us trouble, as having secretly carried you off, and so we should be compelled either to lose all our property, or a very large sum, or to suffer something else besides this? For, if you fear anything of the kind, dismiss your fears; for we are justified in running the risk to save you—and, if need be, even a greater risk than this. But be persuaded by me, and do not refuse.

Socr. I am anxious about this, Crito, and about many other things.

Cri. Do not fear this, however; for the sum is not large on receipt of which certain persons are willing to save you, and take you hence. In the next place, do you not see how cheap these informers are, so that there would be no need of a large sum for them? My fortune is at your service, sufficient, I think, for the purpose; then if, out of regard to me, you do not think right to spend my money, these strangers here are ready to spend theirs. One of them, Simmias the Theban, has brought with him a sufficient sum for the very purpose. Cebes, too, is ready, and very many others. So that, as I said, do not, through fears of this kind, hesitate to save yourself, nor let what you said in court give you any trouble, that if you went from hence you would not know what to do with yourself. For in many places, and wherever you go, men will love you; and if you are disposed to go to Thessaly, I have friends there who will esteem you very highly, and will insure your safety, so that no one in Thessaly will molest you.

Moreover, Socrates, you do not appear to me to pursue a just course in giving yourself up when you might be saved; and you press on the very results with respect to yourself which your enemies would press, and have pressed, in their anxiety to destroy you. Besides this, too, you appear to me to betray your own sons, whom, when it is in your power to rear and educate them, you will abandon, and, so far as you are concerned, they will meet with such a fate as chance brings them, and, as is probable, they will meet with such things as orphans are wont to experience in a state of orphanage. Surely one ought not to have children, or one should go through the toil of rearing and instructing them. But you appear to me to have chosen the most indolent course; though you ought to have chosen such a course as a good and brave man would have done, since you profess to have made virtue your study through the whole of your life; so that I am ashamed both for you and for us who are your friends, lest this whole affair of yours should seem to be the effect of cowardice on our part—your appearing to stand your trial in the court, since you appeared when it was in your power not to have done so, the very manner in which the trial was conducted, and this last circumstance, as it were, a ridiculous consummation of the whole business; your appearing to have escaped from us through our indolence and cowardice, who did not save you; nor did you save yourself, when it was practicable and possible, had we but exerted ourselves a little. Think of these things, therefore, Socrates, and beware, lest, besides the evil that will result, they be disgraceful both to you and to us; advise, then, with yourself; though, indeed, there is no longer time for advising—your resolve should be already made. And there is but one plan; for in the following night the whole must be accomplished. If we delay, it will be impossible and no longer practicable. By all means, therefore, Socrates, be persuaded by me, and on no account refuse.

Socr. My dear Crito, your zeal would be very commendable were it united with right principle; otherwise, by how much the more earnest it is, by so much is it the more sad. We must consider, therefore, whether this plan should be adopted or not. For I not now only, but always, am a person who will obey nothing within me but reason, according as it appears to me on mature deliberation to be best. And the reasons which I formerly professed I cannot now reject, because this misfortune has befallen me; but they appear to me in much the same light, and I respect and honor them as before; so that if we are unable to adduce any better at the present time, be assured that I shall not give in to you, even though the power of the multitude should endeavor to terrify us like children, by threatening more than it does now, bonds and death, and confiscation of property. How, therefore, may we consider the matter most conveniently? First of all, if we recur to the argument which you used about opinions, whether on former occasions it was rightly resolved or not, that we ought to pay attention to some opinions, and to others not; or whether, before it was necessary that I should die, it was rightly resolved; but now it has become clear that it was said idly for argument's sake, though in reality it was merely jest and trifling. I desire then, Crito, to consider, in common with you, whether it will appear to me in a different light, now that I am in this condition, or the same, and whether we shall give it up or yield to it. It was said, I think, on former occasions, by those who were thought to speak seriously, as I just now observed, that of the opinions which men entertain some should be very highly esteemed and others not. By the gods! Crito, does not this appear to you to be well said? For you, in all human probability, are out of all danger of dying to-morrow, and the present calamity will not lead your judgment astray. Consider, then; does it not appear to you to have been rightly settled that we ought not to respect all the opinions of men, but some we should, and others not? Nor yet the opinions of all men, but of some we should, and of others not? What say you? Is not this rightly resolved?

Cri. It is.

Socr. Therefore we should respect the good, but not the bad?

Cri. Yes.

Socr. And are not the good those of the wise, and the bad those of the foolish?

Cri. How can it be otherwise?

Socr. Come, then: how, again, were the following points settled? Does a man who practices gymnastic exercises and applies himself to them, pay attention to the praise and censure and opinion of everyone, or of that one man only who happens to be a physician, or teacher of the exercises?

Cri. Of that one only.

Socr. He ought, therefore, to fear the censures and covet the praises of that one, but not those of the multitude.

Cri. Clearly.

Socr. He ought, therefore, so to practice and exercise himself, and to eat and drink, as seems fitting to the one who presides and knows, rather than to all others together.

Cri. It is so.

Socr. Well, then, if he disobeys the one, and disregards his opinion and praise, but respects that of the multitude and of those who know nothing, will he not suffer some evil?

Cri. How should he not?

Socr. But what is this evil? Whither does it tend, and on what part of him that disobeys will it fall?

Cri. Clearly on his body, for this it ruins.

Socr. You say well. The case is the same, too, Crito, with all other things, not to go through them all. With respect then, to things just and unjust, base and honorable, good and evil, about which we are now consulting, ought we to follow the opinion of the multitude, and to respect it, or that of one, if there is anyone who understands, whom we ought to reverence and respect rather than all others together? And if we do not obey him, shall we not corrupt and injure that part of ourselves which becomes better by justice, but is ruined by injustice? Or is this nothing?

Cri. I agree with you, Socrates.

Socr. Come, then, if we destroy that which becomes better by what is wholesome, but is impaired by what is unwholesome, through being persuaded by those who do not understand, can we enjoy life when that is impaired? And this is the body we are speaking of, is it not?

Cri. Yes.

Socr. Can we, then, enjoy life with a diseased and impaired body?

Cri. By no means.

Socr. But can we enjoy life when that is impaired which injustice ruins but justice benefits? Or do we think that to be of less value than the body, whatever part of us it may be, about which injustice and justice are concerned'

Cri. By no means.

Socr. But of more value?

Cri. Much more.

Socr. We must not then, my excellent friend, so much regard what the multitude will say of us, but what he will say who understands the just and the unjust, the one, even truth itself. So that at first you did not set out with a right principle, when you laid it down that we ought to regard the opinion of the multitude with respect to things just and honorable and good, and their contraries. However, someone may say, are not the multitude able to put us to death?

Cri. This, too, is clear, Socrates, anyone might say so.

Socr. You say truly. But, my admirable friend, this principle which we have just discussed appears to me to be the same as it was before[10]. And consider this, moreover, whether it still holds good with us or not, that we are not to be anxious about living but about living well.

Cri. It does hold good.

Socr. And does this hold good or not, that to live well and Honorable and justly are the same thing?

Cri. It does.

Socr. From what has been admitted, then, this consideration arises, whether it is just or not that I should endeavor to leave this place without the permission of the Athenians. And should it appear to be just, we will make the attempt, but if not, we will give it up. But as to the considerations which you mention, of an outlay of money, reputation, and the education of children, beware, Crito, lest such considerations as these in reality belong to these multitudes, who rashly put one to death, and would restore one to life, if they could do so, without any reason at all. But we, since reason so requires, must consider nothing else than what we just now mentioned, whether we shall act justly in paying money and contracting obligations to those who will lead me hence, as well they who lead me as we who are led hence, or whether, in truth, we shall not act unjustly in doing all these things. And if we should appear in so doing to be acting unjustly, observe that we must not consider whether from remaining here and continuing quiet we must needs die, or suffer anything else, rather than whether we shall be acting unjustly.

Cri. You appear to me to speak wisely, Socrates, but see what we are to do.

Socr. Let us consider the matter together, my friend, and if you have anything to object to what I say, make good your objection, and I will yield to you, but if not, cease, my excellent friend, to urge upon me the same thing so often, that I ought to depart hence against the will of the Athenians. For I highly esteem your endeavors to persuade me thus to act, so long as it is not against my will Consider, then, the beginning of our inquiry, whether it is stated to your entire satisfaction, and endeavor to answer the question put to you exactly as you think right.

35

Cri. I will endeavor to do so.

Socr. Say we, then, that we should on no account deliberately commit injustice, or may we commit injustice under certain circumstances, under others not? Or is it on no account either good or honorable to commit injustice, as we have often agreed on former occasions, and as we just now said? Or have all those our former admissions been dissipated in these few days, and have we, Crito, old men as we are, been for a long time seriously conversing with each other without knowing that we in no respect differ from children? Or does the case, beyond all question, stand as we then determined? Whether the multitude allow it or not, and whether we must suffer a more severe or a milder punishment than this, still is injustice on every account both evil and disgraceful to him who commits it? Do we admit this, or not?

Cri. We do admit it.

Socr. On no account, therefore, ought we to act unjustly.

Cri. Surely not.

Socr. Neither ought one who is injured to return the injury, as the multitude think, since it is on no account right to act unjustly.

Cri. It appears not.

Socr. What, then? Is it right to do evil, Crito, or not?

Cri. Surely it is not right, Socrates.

Socr. But what? To do evil in return when one has been evil-entreated, is that right, or not?

Cri. By no means.

Socr. For to do evil to men differs in no respect from committing injustice.

Cri. You say truly.

Socr. It is not right, therefore, to return an injury, or to do evil to any man, however one may have suffered from him. But take care, Crito, that in allowing these things you do not allow them contrary to your opinion, for I know that to some few only these things both do appear, and will appear, to be true. They, then, to whom these things appear true, and they to whom they do not, have no sentiment in common, and must needs despise each other, while they look to each other's opinions. Consider well, then, whether you coincide and think with me, and whether we can begin our deliberations from this point—that it is never right either to do an injury or to return an injury, or when one has been evil-entreated, to revenge one's self by doing evil in return, or do you dissent from, and not coincide in this principle? For so it appears to me, both long since and now, but if you in any respect think otherwise, say so and inform me. But if you persist in your former opinions, hear what follows.

Cri. I do persist in them, and think with you. Speak on, then.

Socr. I say next, then, or rather I ask; whether when a man has promised to do things that are just he ought to do them, or evade his promise?

Cri. He ought to do them.

Socr. Observe, then, what follows. By departing hence without the leave of the city, are we not doing evil to some, and that to those to whom we ought least of all to do it, or not? And do we abide by what we agreed on as being just, or do we not?

Cri. I am unable to answer your question, Socrates; for I do not understand it.

Socr. Then, consider it thus. If, while we were preparing to run away, or by whatever name we should call it, the laws and commonwealth should come, and, presenting themselves before us, should say, "Tell me, Socrates, what do you purpose doing? Do you design anything else by this proceeding in which you are engaged than to destroy us, the laws, and the whole city, so far as you are able? Or do you think it possible for that city any longer to subsist, and not be subverted, in which judgments that are passed have no force, but are set aside and destroyed by private persons?"—what should we say, Crito, to these and similar remonstrances? For anyone, especially an orator, would have much to say on the violation of the law, which enjoins that judgments passed shall be enforced. Shall we say to them that the city has done us an injustice, and not passed a right sentence? Shall we say this, or what else?

Cri. This, by Jupiter! Socrates.

Socr. What, then, if the laws should say, "Socrates, was it not agreed between us that you should abide by the judgments which the city should pronounce?" And if we should wonder at their speaking thus, perhaps they would say, "Wonder not, Socrates, at what we say, but answer, since you are accustomed to make use of questions and answers. For, come, what charge have you against us and the city, that you attempt to destroy us? Did we not first give you being? and did not your father, through us, take your mother to wife and beget you? Say, then, do you find fault with those laws among us that relate to marriage as being bad?" I should say, "I do not find fault with them." "Do you with those that relate to your nurture when born, and the education with which you were instructed? Or did not the laws, ordained on this point, enjoin rightly, in requiring your father to instruct you in music and gymnastic exercises?" I should say, rightly. Well, then, since you were born, nurtured, and educated through our means, can you say, first of all, that you are not both our offspring and our slave, as well you as your ancestors? And if this be so, do you think that there are equal rights between us? and whatever we attempt to do to you, do you think you may justly do to us in turn? Or had you not equal rights with your father, or master, if you happened to have one, so as to return what you suffered, neither to retort when found fault with, nor, when stricken, to strike again, nor many other things of the kind; but that with your country and the laws you may do so; so that if we attempt to destroy you, thinking it to be just, you also should endeavor, so far as you are able, in return, to destroy us, the laws, and your country; and in doing this will you say that you act justly—you who, in reality, make virtue your chief object? Or are you so wise as not to know that one's country is more honorable, venerable, and sacred, and more highly prized both by gods, and men possessed of understanding, than mother and father, and all other progenitors; and that one ought to reverence, submit to, and appease one's country, when angry, rather than one's father; and either persuade it or do what it orders, and to suffer quietly if it bids one suffer, whether to be beaten, or put in bonds; or if it sends one out to battle there to be wounded or slain, this must be done; for justice so requires, and one must not give way, or retreat, or leave one's post; but that both in war and in a court of justice, and everywhere one must do what one's city and country enjoin, or persuade it in such manner as justice allows; but that to offer violence either to one's mother or father is not holy, much less to one's country? What shall we say to these things, Crito? That the laws speak the truth, or not?

Cri. It seems so to me.

Socr. "Consider, then, Socrates," the laws perhaps might say, "whether we say truly that in what you are now attempting you are attempting to do what is not just toward us. For we, having given you birth, nurtured, instructed you, and having imparted to you and all other citizens all the good in our power, still proclaim, by giving the power to every Athenian who pleases, when he has arrived at years of discretion, and become acquainted with the business of the state, and us, the laws, that anyone who is not satisfied with us may take his property, and go wherever he pleases. And if anyone of you wishes to go to a colony, if he is not satisfied with us and the city, or to migrate and settle in another country, none of us, the laws, hinder or forbid him going whithersoever he pleases, taking with him all his property. But whoever continues with us after he has seen the manner in which we administer justice, and in other respects govern the city, we now say that he has in fact entered into a compact with us to do what we order; and we affirm that he who does not obey is in three respects guilty of injustice—because he does not obey us who gave him being, and because he does not obey us who nurtured him, and because, having made a compact that he would obey us, he neither does so, nor does he persuade us if we do anything wrongly; though we propose for his consideration, and do not rigidly command him to do what we order, but leave him the choice of one of two things, either to persuade us, or to do what we require, and yet he does neither of these."

And we say that you, O Socrates! will be subject to these charges if you accomplish your design, and that not least of the Athenians, but most so of all." And if I should ask, "For what reason?" they would probably justly retort on me by saying that, among all the Athenians, I especially made this compact with them. For they would say, "Socrates, we have strong proof of this, that you were satisfied both with us and the city; for, of all the Athenians, you especially would never have dwelt in it if it had not been especially agreeable to you; for you never went out of the city to any of the public spectacles, except once to the Isthmian games, nor anywhere else, except on military service, nor have you ever gone abroad as other men do, nor had you ever had any desire to become acquainted with any other city or other laws, but we and our city were sufficient for you; so strongly were you attached to us, and so far did you consent to submit to our government, both in other respects and in begetting children in this city, in consequence of your being satisfied with it. Moreover, in your very trial, it was in your power to have imposed on yourself a sentence of exile, if you pleased, and might then have done, with the consent of the city, what you now attempt against its consent. Then, indeed, you boasted yourself as not being grieved if you must needs die; but you preferred, as you said, death to exile. Now, however, you are neither ashamed of those professions, nor do you revere us, the laws, since you endeavor to destroy us, and you act as the vilest slave would act, by endeavoring to make your escape contrary to the conventions and the compacts by which you engaged to submit to our government. First, then, therefore, answer us this, whether we speak the truth or not in affirming that you agreed to be governed by us in deed, though not in word?" What shall we say to this, Crito? Can we do otherwise than assent?

Cri. We must needs do so, Socrates.

Socr. "What else, then," they will say, "are you doing but violating the conventions and compacts which you made with us, though you did not enter into them from compulsion or through deception, or from being compelled to determine in a short time but during the space of seventy years, in which you might have departed if you had been dissatisfied with us, and the compacts had not appeared to you to be just? You, however, preferred neither Laced詢on nor Crete, which you several times said are governed by good laws, nor any other of the Grecian or barbarian cities; but you have been less out of Athens than the lame and the blind, and other maimed persons. So much, it is evident, were you satisfied with the city and us, the laws, beyond the rest of the Athenians; for who can be satisfied with a city without laws? But now will you not abide by your compacts? You will, if you are persuaded by us, Socrates, and will not make yourself ridiculous by leaving the city."

"For consider, by violating these compacts and offending against any of them, what good you will do to yourself or your friends. For that your friends will run the risk of being themselves banished, and deprived of the rights of citizenship, or of forfeiting their property, is pretty clear. And as for yourself, if you should go to one of the neighboring cities, either Thebes or Megara, for both are governed by good laws, you will go there, Socrates, as an enemy to their polity; and such as have any regard for their country will look upon you with suspicion, regarding you as a corrupter of the laws; and you will confirm the opinion of the judges, so that they will appear to have condemned you rightly, for whose is a corrupter of the laws will appear in all likelihood to be a corrupter of youths and weak-minded men. Will you, then, avoid these well-governed cities, and the best-ordered men? And should you do so, will it be worth your while to live? Or will you approach them, and have the effrontery to converse with them, Socrates, on subjects the same as you did here—that virtue and justice, legal institutions and laws, should be most highly valued by men? And do you not think that this conduct of Socrates would be very indecorous? You must think so. But you will keep clear of these places, and go to Thessaly, to Crito's friends, for there are the greatest disorder and licentiousness; and perhaps they will gladly hear you relating how drolly you escaped from prison, clad in some dress or covered with a skin, or in some other disguise such as fugitives are wont to dress themselves in, having so changed your usual appearance. And will no one say that you, though an old man, with but a short time to live, in all probability, have dared to have such a base desire of life as to violate the most sacred laws? Perhaps not, should you not offend anyone. But if you should, you will hear, Socrates, manythings utterly unworthy of you. You will live, too, in a state of abject dependence on all men, and as their slave. But what will you do in Thessaly besides feasting, as if you had gone to Thessaly to a banquet? And what will become of those discourses about justice and all other virtues? But do you wish to live for the sake of your children, that you may rear and educate them? What then? Will you take them to Thessaly, and there rear and educate them, making them aliens to their country, that they may owe you this obligation too? Or, if not so, being reared here, will they be better reared and educated while you are living, though not with them, for your friends will take care of them? Whether, if you go to Thessaly, will they take care of them, but if you go to Hades will they not take care of them? If, however, any advantage is to be derived from those that say they are your friends, we must think they will."

"Then, O Socrates! be persuaded by us who have nurtured you, and do not set a higher value on your children, or on life, or on anything else than justice, that, when you arrive in Hades, you may have all this to say in your defense before those who have dominion there. For neither here in this life, if you do what is proposed, does it appear to be better, or more just, or more holy to yourself, or any of your friends; nor will it be better for you when you arrive there. But now you depart, if you do depart, unjustly treated, not by us, the laws, but by men; but should you escape, having thus disgracefully returned injury for injury, and evil for evil, having violated your own compacts and conventions which you made with us, and having done evil to those to whom you least of all should have done it—namely, yourself, your friends, your country, and us—both we shall be indignant with you as long as you live, and there our brothers, the laws in Hades, will not receive you favorably knowing that you attempted, so far as you were able, to destroy us. Let not Crito, then, persuade you to do what he advises, rather than we."

These things, my dear friend Crito, be assured, I seem to hear as the votaries of Cybele[11] seem to hear the flutes. And the sound of these words booms in my ear, and makes me incapable of hearing anything else. Be sure, then, so long as I retain my present opinions, if you should say anything contrary to these, you will speak in vain. If, however, you think that you can prevail at all, say on.

Cri. But, Socrates, I have nothing to say.

Socr. Desist, then, Crito, and let us pursue this course, since this way the deity leads us.

Footnotes

[6] See the Phædo sec 1.

[7] A promontory at the southern extremity of Attica

[8] The Eleven

[9] See Homer's "Iliad," 1 IX, v 363

[10] That is to say, the principle which we had laid down in former discussions that no regard is to be had to popular opinion, is still found to hold good.

[11] The Corybantes, priests of Cybele, who in their solemn festivals made such a noise with flutes that the hearers could hear no other sound.

Introduction to the Phaeodo

This dialogue presents us with an account of the manner In which Socrates spent the last day of his, life, and how he met his death. The main subject is that of the soul's immortality, which Socrates takes upon himself to prove with as much certainty as it is possible for the human mind to arrive at. The question itself, though none could be better suited to the occasion, arises simply and naturally from the general conversation that precedes it.

When his friends visit him in the morning for the purpose of spending this his last day with him, they find him sitting up in bed, and rubbing his leg, which had just been freed from bonds. He remarks on the unaccountable alternation and connection between pleasure and pain, and adds that Aesop, had he observed it, would have made a fable from it. This remark reminds Cebes of Socrates's having put some of Aesop's fables into metre since his imprisonment, and he asks, for the satisfaction of the poet Evenus, what has induced him to do so. Socrates explains his reason, and concludes by bidding him tell Evenus to follow him as soon as he can. Simmias expresses his surprise at this message, on which Socrates asks, "Is not Evenus a philosopher?" and on the question being answered in the affirmative, he says that he or any philosopher would be willing to die, though perhaps he would not commit violence on himself. This, again, seems a contradiction to Simmias; but Socrates explains it by showing that our souls are placed in the body by God, and may not leave it without his permission. Whereupon Cebes objects that in that case foolish men only would wish to die, and quit the service of the best of masters, to which Simmias agrees. Socrates, therefore, proposes to plead his case before them, and to show that there is a great probability that after this life he shall go into the presence of God and good men, and be happy in proportion to the purity of his own mind.

He begins[12] by stating that philosophy itself is nothing else than a preparation for and meditation on death. Death and philosophy have this in common: death separates the soul from the body; philosophy draws off the mind from bodily things to the contemplation of truth and virtue: for he is not a true philosopher who is led away by bodily pleasures, since the senses are the source of ignorance and all evil. The mind, therefore, is entirely occupied in meditating on death, and freeing itself as much as possible from the body. How, then, can such a man be afraid of death? He who grieves at the approach of death cannot be a true lover of wisdom, but is a lover of his body. And, indeed, most men are temperate through intemperance; that is to say, they abstain from some pleasures that they may the more easily and permanently enjoy others. They embrace only a shadow of virtue, not virtue itself, since they estimate the value of all things by the pleasures they afford. Whereas the philosopher purifies his mind from all such things, and pursues virtue and wisdom for their own sakes. This course Socrates himself has pursued to the utmost of his ability, with what success he should shortly know; and on these grounds he did not repine at leaving his friends in this world, being persuaded that in another he should meet with good masters and good friends.

Upon this Cebes[13] says that he agrees with all else that had been said, but cannot help entertaining doubts of what will become of the soul when separated from the body, for the common opinion is that it is dispersed and vanishes like breath or smoke, and no longer exists anywhere. Socrates, therefore, proposes to inquire into the probability of the case, a fit employment for him under his present circumstances.

His first argument[14] is drawn from the ancient belief prevalent among men, that souls departing hence exist in Hades, and are produced again from the dead. If this be true, it must follow that our souls are there, for they could not be produced again if they did not exist; and its truth is confirmed by this, that it is a general law of nature that contraries are produced from contraries—the greater from the less, strong from weak, slow from swift, heat from cold, and in like manner life from death, and vice versa. To explain this more clearly, he proceeds to show that what is changed passes from one state to another, and so undergoes three different states—first, the actual state; then the transition; and, thirdly, the new state; as from a state of sleep, by awaking to being awake. In like manner birth is a transition from a state of death to life, and dying from life to death; so that the soul, by the act of dying, only passes to another state. If it were not so, all nature would in time become dead, just as if people did not awake out of sleep all would at last be buried in eternal sleep. Whence the conclusion is that the souls of men are not annihilated by death.

Cebes[15] agrees to this reasoning, and adds that he is further convinced, of its truth by calling to mind an argument used by Socrates on former occasions, that knowledge is nothing but reminiscence; and if this is so, the soul must have existed, and had knowledge, before it became united to the body.

But in case Simmias should not yet be satisfied, Socrates[16] proceeds to enlarge on this, his second argument, drawn from reminiscence. We daily find that we are carried from the knowledge of one thing to another. Things perceived by the eyes, ears, and other senses bring up the thought of other things; thus the sight of a lyre or a garment reminds us of a friend, and not only are we thus reminded of sensible objects, but of things which are comprehended by the mind alone, and have no sensitive existence. For we have formed in our minds an idea of abstract equality, of the beautiful, the just, the good; in short, of everything which we say exists without the aid of the senses, for we use them only in the perception of individual things; whence it follows that the mind did not acquire this knowledge in this life, but must have had it before, and therefore the soul must have existed before.

Simmias and Cebes[17] both agree in admitting that Socrates has proved the pre-existence of the soul, but insist that he has not shown it to be immortal, for that nothing hinders but that, according to the popular opinion, it may be dispersed at the dissolution of the body. To which Socrates replies, that if their former admissions are joined to his last argument, the immortality, as well as the pre-existence, of the soul has been sufficiently proved. For if it is true that anything living is produced from that which is dead, then the soul must exist after death, otherwise it could not be produced again.

However, to remove the apprehension that the soul may be dispersed by a wind, as it were, Socrates proceeds, in his third argument,[18] to examine that doubt more thoroughly. What, then, is meant by being dispersed but being dissolved into its parts? In order, therefore, to a thing being capable of dispersion it must be compounded of parts. Now, there are two kinds of things—one compounded, the other simple The former kind is subject to change, the latter not, and can be comprehended by the mind alone. The one is visible, the other invisible; and the soul, which is invisible, when it employs the bodily senses, wanders and is confused, but when it abstracts itself from the body it attains to the knowledge of that which is eternal, immortal, and unchangeable. The soul, therefore, being uncompounded and invisible, must be indissoluble; that is to say, immortal.

Still Simmias and Cebes[19] are unconvinced. The former objects that the soul, according to Socrates's own showing, is nothing but a harmony resulting from a combination of the parts of the body, and so may perish with the body, as the harmony of a lyre does when the lyre itself is broken. And Cebes, though he admits that the soul is more durable than the body, yet objects that it is not, therefore, of necessity immortal, but may in time wear out; and it is by no means clear that this is not its last period.

These objections produce a powerful effect on the rest of the company; but Socrates, undismayed, exhorts them not to suffer themselves to be deterred from seeking the truth by any difficulties they may meet with; and then proceeds[20] to show, in a moment, the fallacy of Simmias's objection. It was before admitted, he says, that the soul existed before the body; but harmony is produced after the lyre is formed, so that the two cases are totally different. And, further, there are various degrees of harmony, but every soul is as much a soul as any other. But, then, what will a person who holds this doctrine, that the soul is harmony, say of virtue and vice in the soul? Will he call them another kind of harmony and discord? If so, he will contradict himself; for it is admitted that one soul is not more or less a soul than another, and therefore one cannot be more or less harmonized than another, and one could not admit of a greater degree of virtue or vice than another; and indeed a soul, being harmony, could not partake of vice at all, which is discord.

Socrates, having thus satisfactorily answered the argument adduced by Simmias, goes on to rebut that of Cebes,[21] who objected that the soul might in time wear out. In order to do this, he relates that, when a young man, he attempted to investigate the causes of all things, why they exist and why they perish; and in the course of his researches, finding the futility of attributing the existence of things to what are called natural causes, he resolved on endeavoring to find out the reasons of things. He therefore assumed that there are a certain abstract beauty and goodness and magnitude, and so of all other things; the truth of which being granted, he thinks he shall be able to prove that the soul is immortal.

This, then, being conceded by Cebes, Socrates[22] argues that everything that is beautiful is so from partaking of abstract beauty, and great from partaking of magnitude, and little from partaking of littleness. Now, it is impossible, he argues, that contraries can exist in the same thing at the same time; for instance, the same thing cannot possess both magnitude and littleness, but one will withdraw at the approach of the other; and not only so, but things which, though not contrary to each other, yet always contain contraries within themselves, cannot co-exist; for instance, the number three has no contrary, yet it contains within itself the idea of odd, which is the contrary of even, and so three never can become even; in like manner, heat while it is heat can never admit the idea of its contrary, cold. Now, if this method of reasoning is applied to the soul, it will be found to be immortal; for life and death are contraries, and never can co-exist; but wherever the soul is, there is life: so that it contains within itself that which is contrary to death, and consequently can never admit of death; therefore it is immortal.

With this he closes his arguments in support of the soul's immortality. Cebes owns himself convinced, but Simmias, though he is unable to make any objection to the soundness of Socrates's reasoning, cannot help still entertaining doubts on the subject. If, however, the soul is immortal, Socrates proceeds,[23] great need is there in this life to endeavor to become as wise and good as possible. For if death were a deliverance from everything, it would be a great gain for the wicked; but since the soul appears to be immortal, it must go to the place suited to its nature. For it is said that each person's demon conducts him to a place where he receives sentence according to his deserts.

He then[24] draws a fanciful picture of the various regions of the earth, to which the good and the bad will respectively go after death, and exhorts his friends to use every endeavor to acquire virtue and wisdom in this life, "for," he adds, "the reward is noble, and the hope great."

Having thus brought his subject to a conclusion, Socrates proposes to bathe himself, in order not to trouble others to wash his dead body. Crito thereupon asks if he has any commands to give, and especially how he would be buried, to which he, with his usual cheerfulness, makes answer, "Just as you please, if only you can catch me;" and then, smiling, he reminds them that after death he shall be no longer with them, and begs the others of the party to be sureties to Crito for his absence from the body, as they had been before bound for his presence before his judges.

After he had bathed, and taken leave of his children and the women of his family the officer of the Eleven comes in to intimate to him that it is now time to drink the poison. Crito urges a little delay, as the sun had not yet set; but Socrates refuses to make himself ridiculous by showing such a fondness for life. The man who is to administer the poison is therefore sent for; and on his holding out the cup, Socrates, neither trembling nor changing color or countenance at all, but, as he was wont, looking steadfastly at the man, asked if he might make a libation to anyone; and being told that no more poison than enough had been mixed, he simply prayed that his departure from this to another world might be happy, and then drank off the poison, readily and calmly. His friends, who had hitherto with difficulty restrained themselves, could no longer control the outward expressions of grief, to which Socrates said, "What are you doing, my friends? I, for this reason, chiefly, sent away the women, that they might not commit any folly of this kind; for I have heard that it is right to die with good omens. Be quiet, therefore, and bear up."

When he had walked about for a while his legs began to grow heavy, so he lay down on his back; and his body, from the feet upward, gradually grew cold and stiff. His last words were, "Crito, we owe a cock to Æsculapius; pay it, therefore, and do not neglect it."

"This," concludes Phædo, "was the end of our friend—a man, as we may say, the best of all his time, that we have known, and, moreover, the most wise and just."

Footnotes

[12] Sec. 21-39.
[13] Sec. 39, 40.
[14] Sec. 40-46.
[15] Sec. 47.
[16] Sec. 48-57.
[17] Sec. 55-59.
[18] Sec. 61-75.
[19] Sec. 76-84.
[20] Sec. 93-99.
[21] Sec. 100-112.
[22] Sec. 112-128.
[23] Sec. 129-131.
[24] Sec. 132-145.

Phaedo; Or, the Immortality of the Soul

FIRST ECHECRATES, PHAEDO. THEN SOCRATES, APOLLODORUS, CEBES, SIMMIAS, AND CRITO.

Ech. Were you personally present, Phædo, with Socrates on that day when he drank the poison in prison, or did you hear an account of it from someone else?

Phaedo. I was there myself, Echecrates.

Ech. What, then, did he say before his death, and how did he die? for I should be glad to hear: for scarcely any citizen of Phlius[25] ever visits Athens now, nor has any stranger for a long time come from thence who was able to give us a clear account of the particulars, except that he had died from drinking poison; but he was unable to tell us anything more.

Phaedo. And did you not hear about the trial—how it went off?

Ech. Yes; someone told me this; and I wondered that, as it took place so long ago, he appears to have died long afterward. What was the reason of this, Phædo?

Phaedo. An accidental circumstance happened in his favor, Echecrates; for the poop of the ship which the Athenians send to Delos chanced to be crowned on the day before the trial.

Ech. But what is this ship?

Phaedo. It is the ship, as the Athenians say, in which Theseus formerly conveyed the fourteen boys and girls to Crete, and saved both them and himself. They, therefore, made a vow to Apollo on that occasion, as it is said, that if they were saved they would every year dispatch a solemn embassy to Delos; which, from that time to the present, they send yearly to the god.

When they begin the preparations for this solemn embassy, they have a law that the city shall be purified during this period, and that no public execution shall take place until the ship has reached Delos, and returned to Athens; and this occasionally takes a long time, when the winds happen to impede their passage. The commencement of the embassy is when the priest of Apollo has crowned the poop of the ship. And this was done, as I said, on the day before the trial: on this account Socrates had a long interval in prison between the trial and his death.

Ech. And what, Phædo, were the circumstances of his death? What was said and done? and who of his friends were with him? or would not the magistrates allow them to be present, but did he die destitute of friends?

Phaedo. By no means; but some, indeed several, were present.

Ech. Take the trouble, then, to relate to me all the particulars as clearly as you can, unless you have any pressing business.

Phaedo. I am at leisure, and will endeavor to give you a full account; for to call Socrates to mind, whether speaking myself or listening to someone else, is always most delightful to me.

Ech. And indeed, Phædo, you have others to listen to you who are of the same mind. However, endeavor to relate everything as accurately as you can.

Phaedo. I was, indeed, wonderfully affected by being present, for I was not impressed with a feeling of pity, like one present at the death of a friend; for the man appeared to me to be happy, Echecrates, both from his manner and discourse, so fearlessly and nobly did he meet his death: so much so, that it occurred to me that in going to Hades he was not going without a divine destiny, but that when he arrived there he would be happy, if anyone ever was. For this reason I was entirely uninfluenced by any feeling of pity, as would seem likely to be the case with one present on so mournful an occasion; nor was I affected by pleasure from being engaged in philosophical discussions, as was our custom; for our conversation was of that kind. But an altogether unaccountable feeling possessed me, a kind of unusual mixture compounded of pleasure and pain together, when I considered that he was immediately about to die. And all of us who were present were affected in much the same manner, at one time laughing, at another weeping—one of us especially, Apollodorus, for you know the man and his manner.

Ech. How should I not?

Phaedo. He, then, was entirely overcome by these emotions; and I, too, was troubled, as well as the others.

Ech. But who were present, Phædo?

Phaedo. Of his fellow-countrymen, this Apollodorus was present, and Critobulus, and his father, Crito; moreover, Hermogenes, Epigenes, Æschines and Antisthenes; Ctesippus the Pæanian, Menexenus, and some others of his countrymen, were also there: Plato, I think, was sick.

Ech. Were any strangers present?

Phaedo. Yes; Simmias, the Theban, Cebes and Phædondes; and from Megara, Euclides and Terpsion.

7. Ech. But what! were not Aristippus and Cleombrotus present?

Phaedo. No, for they were said to be at Ægina.

Ech. Was anyone else there?

Phaedo. I think that these were nearly all who were present.

Ech. Well, now, what do you say was the subject of conversation?

Phaedo. I will endeavor to relate the whole to you from the beginning. On the preceding days I and the others were constantly in the habit of visiting Socrates, meeting early in the morning at the court house where the trial took place, for it was near the prison.

Here, then, we waited every day till the prison was opened, conversing with each other, for it was not opened very early; but as soon as it was opened we went in to Socrates, and usually spent the day with him. On that occasion, however, we met earlier than usual; for on the preceding day, when we left the prison in the evening, we heard that the ship had arrived from Delos. We therefore urged each other to come as early as possible to the accustomed place. Accordingly we came; and the porter, who used to admit us, coming out, told us to wait, and not to enter until he had called us. "For," he said, "the Eleven are now freeing Socrates from his bonds, and announcing to him that he must die to-day." But in no long time he returned, and bade us enter.

When we entered, we found Socrates just freed from his bonds, and Xantippe, you know her, holding his little boy, and sitting by him. As soon as Xantippe saw us she wept aloud, and said such things as women usually do on such occasions—as, "Socrates, your friends will now converse with you for the last time, and you with them." But Socrates, looking towards Crito, said: "Crito, let someone take her home." Upon which some of Crito's attendants led her away, wailing and beating herself.

But Socrates, sitting up in bed, drew up his leg, and rubbed it with his hand, and as he rubbed it, said: "What an unaccountable thing, my friends, that seems to be, which men call pleasure! and how wonderfully is it related toward that which appears to be its contrary, pain, in that they will not both be present to a man at the same time! Yet if anyone pursues and attains the one, he is almost always compelled to receive the other, as if they were both united together from one head."

"And it seems to me," he said, "that if Aesop had observed this he would have made a fable from it, how the deity, wishing to reconcile these warring principles, when he could not do so, united their heads together, and from hence whomsoever the one visits the other attends immediately after; as appears to be the case with me, since I suffered pain in my leg before from the chain, but now pleasure seems to have succeeded."

Hereupon Cebes, interrupting him, said: "By Jupiter! Socrates, you have done well in reminding me; with respect to the poems which you made, by putting into metre those Fables of Aesop and the hymn to Apollo, several other persons asked me, and especially Evenus recently, with what design you made them after you came here, whereas before you had never made any.

If therefore, you care at all that I should be able to answer Evenus, when he asks me again—for I am sure he will do so—tell me what I must say to him."

"Tell him the truth, then, Cebes," he replied, "that I did not make them from a wish to compete with him, or his poems, for I knew that this would be no easy matter; but that I might discover the meaning of certain dreams, and discharge my conscience, if this should happen to be the music which they have often ordered me to apply myself to. For they were to the following purport: often in my past life the same dream visited me, appearing at different times in different forms, yet always saying the same thing—'Socrates,' it said, 'apply yourself to and practice music.'

And I formerly supposed that it exhorted and encouraged me to continue the pursuit I was engaged in, as those who cheer on racers, so that the dream encouraged me to continue the pursuit I was engaged in—namely, to apply myself to music, since philosophy is the highest music, and I was devoted to it. But now since my trial took place, and the festival of the god retarded my death, it appeared to me that if by chance the dream so frequently enjoined me to apply myself to popular music, I ought not to disobey it, but do so, for that it would be safer for me not to depart hence before I had discharged my conscience by making some poems in obedience to the dream. Thus, then, I first of all composed a hymn to the god whose festival was present; and after the god, considering that a poet, if he means to be a poet, ought to make fables, and not discourses, and knowing that I was not skilled in making fables, I therefore put into verse those Fables of Aesop, which were at hand, and were known to me, and which first occurred to me."

"Tell this, then, to Evenus, Cebes, and bid him farewell, and if he is wise, to follow me as soon as he can. But I depart, as it seems, to-day; for so the Athenians order."

To this Simmias said, "What is this, Socrates, which you exhort Evenus to do? for I often meet with him; and, from what I know of him, I am pretty certain that he will not at all be willing to comply with your advice."

"What, then," said he, "is not Evenus a philosopher?"

"To me he seems to be so," said Simmias.

"Then he will be willing," rejoined Socrates, "and so will everyone who worthily engages in this study. Perhaps, indeed, he will not commit violence on himself; for that, they say, is not allowable." And as he said this he let down his leg from the bed on the ground, and in this posture continued during the remainder of the discussion.

Cebes then asked him, "What do you mean, Socrates, by saying that it is not lawful to commit violence on one's self, but that a philosopher should be willing to follow one who is dying?"

"What, Cebes! have not you and Simmias, who have conversed familiarly with Philolaus[26] on this subject, heard?"

"Nothing very clearly, Socrates."

"I, however, speak only from hearsay; what, then, I have heard I have no scruple in telling. And perhaps it is most becoming for one who is about to travel there to inquire and speculate about the journey thither, what kind we think it is. What else can one do in the interval before sunset?"

"Why, then, Socrates, do they say that it is not allowable to kill one's self? for I, as you asked just now, have heard both Philolaus, when he lived with us, and several others, say that it was not right to do this; but I never heard anything clear upon the subject from anyone."

"Then, you should consider it attentively," said Socrates, "for perhaps you may hear. Probably, however, it will appear wonderful to you, if this alone, of all other things, is a universal truth,[27] and it never happens to a man, as is the case in all other things, that at some times and to some persons only it is better to die than to live; yet that these men for whom it is better to die—this probably will appear wonderful to you—may not without impiety do this good to themselves, but must await another benefactor."

Then Cebes, gently smiling, said, speaking in his own dialect,[28] "Jove be witness!"

"And, indeed," said Socrates, "it would appear to be unreasonable; yet still, perhaps, it has some reason on its side. The maxim, indeed, given on this subject in the mystical doctrines,[29] that we men are in a kind of prison, and that we ought not to free ourselves from it and escape, appears to me difficult to be understood, and not easy to penetrate. This, however, appears to me, Cebes, to be well said: that the gods take care of us, and that we men are one of their possessions. Does it not seem so to you?"

"It does," replied Cebes.

"Therefore," said he, "if one of your slaves were to kill himself, without your having intimated that you wished him to die, should you not be angry with him, and should you not punish him if you could?"

"Certainly," he replied.

"Perhaps, then, in this point of view, it is not unreasonable to assert that a man ought not to kill himself before the deity lays him under a necessity of doing so, such as that now laid on me."

"This, indeed," said Cebes, "appears to be probable. But what you said just now, Socrates, that philosophers should be very willing to die, appears to be an absurdity, if what we said just now is agreeable to reason—that it is God who takes care of us, and that we are his property. For that the wisest men should not be grieved at leaving that service in which they govern them who are the best of all masters—namely, the gods—is not consistent with reason; for surely he cannot think that he will take better care of himself when he has become free. But a foolish man might perhaps think thus, that he should fly from his master, and would not reflect that he ought not to fly from a good one, but should cling to him as much as possible; therefore he would fly against all reason; but a man of sense would desire to be constantly with one better than himself. Thus, Socrates, the contrary of what you just now said is likely to be the case; for it becomes the wise to be grieved at dying, but the foolish to rejoice."

Socrates, on hearing this, appeared to me to be pleased with the pertinacity of Cebes, and, looking toward us, said, "Cebes, you see, always searches out arguments, and is not at all willing to admit at once anything one has said."

Whereupon Simmias replied, "But, indeed, Socrates, Cebes appears to me now to say something to the purpose; for with what design should men really wise fly from masters who are better than themselves, and so readily leave them? And Cebes appears to me to direct his argument against you, because you so easily endure to abandon both us and those good rulers, as you yourself confess, the gods."

"You speak justly," said Socrates, "for I think you mean that I ought to make my defense to this charge, as if I were in a court of justice."

"Certainly," replied Simmias.

"Come, then," said he, "I will endeavor to defend myself more successfully before you than before the judges. For," he proceeded, "Simmias and Cebes, if I did not think that I should go, first of all, among other deities who are both wise and good, and, next, among men who have departed this life, better than any here, I should be wrong in not grieving at death; but now, be assured, I hope to go among good men, though I would not positively assert it. That, however, I shall go among gods who are perfectly good masters, be assured I can positively assert this, if I can anything of the kind. So that, on this account, I am not so much troubled, but I entertain a good hope that something awaits those who die, and that, as was said long since, it will be far better for the good than the evil."

"What, then, Socrates," said Simmias, "would you go away keeping this persuasion to yourself, or would you impart it to us? For this good appears to me to be also common to us; and at the same time it will be an apology for you, if you can persuade us to believe what you say."

"I will endeavor to do so," he said. "But first let us attend to Crito here, and see what it is he seems to have for some time wished to say."

"What else, Socrates," said Crito, "but what he who is to give you the poison told me some time ago, that I should tell you to speak as little as possible? For he says that men become too much heated by speaking, and that nothing of this kind ought to interfere with the poison; and that, otherwise, those who did so were sometimes compelled to drink two or three times."

To which Socrates replied, "Let him alone, and let him attend to his own business, and prepare to give it me twice, or, if occasion require, even thrice."

"I was almost certain what you would say," answered Crito, "but he has been some time pestering me."

"Never mind him," he rejoined.

"But now I wish to render an account to you, my judges, of the reason why a man who has really devoted his life to philosophy, when he is about to die, appears to me, on good grounds, to have confidence, and to entertain a firm hope that the greatest good will befall him in the other world when he has departed this life. How, then, this comes to pass, Simmias and Cebes, I will endeavor to explain."

"For as many as rightly apply themselves to philosophy seem to have left all others in ignorance, that they aim at nothing else than to die and be dead. If this, then, is true, it would surely be absurd to be anxious about nothing else than this during their whole life, but, when it arrives, to be grieved at what they have been long anxious about and aimed at."

Upon this, Simmias, smiling, said, "By Jupiter! Socrates, though I am not now at all inclined to smile, you have made me do so; for I think that the multitude, if they heard this, would think it was very well said in reference to philosophers, and that our countrymen particularly would agree with you, that true philosophers do desire death, and that they are by no means ignorant that they deserve to suffer it."

"And, indeed, Simmias, they would speak the truth, except in asserting that they are not ignorant; for they are ignorant of the sense in which true philosophers desire to die, and in what sense they deserve death, and what kind of death. But," he said, "let us take leave of them, and speak to one another. Do we think that death is anything?"

"Certainly," replied Simmias.

"Is it anything else than the separation of the soul from the body? And is not this to die, for the body to be apart by itself separated from the soul, and for the soul to subsist apart by itself separated from the body? Is death anything else than this?"

54

"No, but this," he replied.

"Consider, then, my good friend, whether you are of the same opinion as I; for thus, I think, we shall understand better the subject we are considering. Does it appear to you to be becoming in a philosopher to be anxious about pleasures, as they are called, such as meats and drinks?"

"By no means, Socrates," said Simmias.

"But what? about the pleasures of love?"

"Not at all."

"What, then? Does such a man appear to you to think other bodily indulgences of value? For instance, does he seem to you to value or despise the possession of magnificent garments and sandals, and other ornaments of the body except so far as necessity compels him to use them?"

"The true philosopher," he answered, "appears to me to despise them."

"Does not, then," he continued, "the whole employment of such a man appear to you to be, not about the body, but to separate himself from it as much as possible, and be occupied about his soul?"

"It does."

"First of all, then, in such matters, does not the philosopher, above all other men, evidently free his soul as much as he can from communion with the body?"

"It appears so."

"And it appears, Simmias, to the generality of men, that he who takes no pleasure in such things, and who does not use them, does not deserve to live; but that he nearly approaches to death who cares nothing for the pleasures that subsist through the body."

"You speak very truly."

"But what with respect to the acquisition of wisdom? Is the body an impediment, or not, if anyone takes it with him as a partner in the search? What I mean is this: Do sight and hearing convey any truth to men, or are they such as the poets constantly sing, who say that we neither hear nor see anything with accuracy? If, however, these bodily senses are neither accurate nor clear, much less can the others be so; for they are all far inferior to these. Do they not seem so to you?"

"Certainly," he replied.

"When, then," said he, "does the soul light on the truth? for when it attempts to consider anything in conjunction with the body, it is plain that it is then led astray by it."

"You say truly."

"Must it not, then, be by reasoning, if at all, that any of the things that really are become known to it?"

"Yes."

"And surely the soul then reasons best when none of these things disturb it—neither hearing, nor sight, nor pain, nor pleasure of any kind; but it retires as much as possible within itself, taking leave of the body; and, so far as it can, not communicating or being in contact with it, it aims at the discovery of that which is."

"Such is the case."

"Does not, then, the soul of the philosopher, in these cases, despise the body, and flee from it, and seek to retire within itself?"

"It appears so."

"But what as to such things as these, Simmias? Do we say that justice itself is something or nothing?"

"We say it is something, by Jupiter!"

"And that beauty and goodness are something?"

"How not?"

"Now, then, have you ever seen anything of this kind with your eyes?"

"By no means," he replied.

"Did you ever lay hold of them by any other bodily sense? But I speak generally, as of magnitude, health, strength and, in a word, of the essence of everything; that is to say, what each is. Is, then, the exact truth of these perceived by means of the body, or is it thus, whoever among us habituates himself to reflect most deeply and accurately on each several thing about which he is considering, he will make the nearest approach to the knowledge of it?"

"Certainly."

"Would not he, then, do this with the utmost purity, who should in the highest degree approach each subject by means of the mere mental faculties, neither employing the sight in conjunction with the reflective faculty, nor introducing any other sense together with reasoning; but who, using pure reflection by itself, should attempt to search out each essence purely by itself, freed as much as possible from the eyes and ears, and, in a word, from the whole body, as disturbing the soul, and not suffering it to acquire truth and wisdom, when it is in communion with it. Is not he the person, Simmias, if anyone can, who will arrive at the knowledge of that which is?"

"You speak with wonderful truth, Socrates," replied Simmias.

"Wherefore," he said, "it necessarily follows from all this that some such opinion as this should be entertained by genuine philosophers, so that they should speak among themselves as follows: 'A by-path, as it were, seems to lead us on in our researches undertaken by reason,' because so long as we are encumbered with the body, and our soul is contaminated with such an evil, we can never fully attain to what we desire; and this, we say, is truth. For the body subjects us to innumerable hinderances on account of its necessary support; and, moreover, if any diseases befall us, they impede us in our search after that which is; and it fills us with longings, desires, fears, all kinds of fancies, and a multitude of absurdities, so that, as it is said in real truth, by reason of the body it is never possible for us to make any advances in wisdom.

For nothing else than the body and its desires occasion wars, seditions, and contests; for all wars among us arise on account of our desire to acquire wealth: and we are compelled to acquire wealth on account of the body, being enslaved to its service; and consequently on all these accounts we are hindered in the pursuit of philosophy. But the worst of all is, that if it leaves us any leisure, and we apply ourselves to the consideration of any subject, it constantly obtrudes itself in the midst of our researches, and occasions trouble and disturbance, and confounds us so that we are not able, by reason of it, to discern the truth. It has, then, in reality been demonstrated to us that if we are ever to know anything purely, we must be separated from the body, and contemplate the things themselves by the mere soul; and then, as it seems, we shall obtain that which we desire, and which we profess ourselves to be lovers of—wisdom—when we are dead, as reason shows, but not while we are alive.

For if it is not possible to know anything purely in conjunction with the body, one of these two things must follow, either that we can never acquire knowledge, or only after we are dead; for then the soul will subsist apart by itself, separate from the body, but not before. And while we live we shall thus, as it seems, approach nearest to knowledge, if we hold no intercourse or communion at all with the body, except what absolute necessity requires, nor suffer ourselves to be polluted by its nature, but purify ourselves from it, until God himself shall release us. And thus being pure, and freed from the folly of body, we shall in all likelihood be with others like ourselves, and shall of ourselves know the whole real essence, and that probably is truth; for it is not allowable for the impure to attain to the pure. Such things, I think, Simmias, all true lovers of wisdom must both think and say to one another. Does it not seem so to you?"

"Most assuredly, Socrates."

"If this, then," said Socrates, "is true, my friend, there is great hope for one who arrives where I am going, there, if anywhere, to acquire that in perfection for the sake of which we have taken so much pains during our past life; so that the journey now appointed me is set out upon with good hope, and will be so by any other man who thinks that his mind has been, as it were, purified."

"Certainly," said Simmias.

"But does not purification consist in this, as was said in a former part of our discourse, in separating as much as possible the soul from the body, and in accustoming it to gather and collect itself by itself on all sides apart from the body, and to dwell, so far as it can, both now and hereafter, alone by itself, delivered, as it were, from the shackles of the body?"

"Certainly," he replied.

"Is this, then, called death, this deliverance and separation of the soul from the body?"

"Assuredly," he answered.

"But, as we affirmed, those who pursue philosophy rightly are especially and alone desirous to deliver it; and this is the very study of philosophers, the deliverance and separation of the soul from the body, is it not?"

"It appears so."

"Then, as I said at first, would it not be ridiculous for a man who has endeavored throughout his life to live as near as possible to death, then, when death arrives, to grieve? would not this be ridiculous?"

"How should it not?"

"In reality, then, Simmias," he continued, "those who pursue philosophy rightly, study to die; and to them, of all men, death is least formidable. Judge from this. Since they altogether hate the body and desire to keep the soul by itself, would it not be irrational if, when this comes to pass, they should be afraid and grieve, and not be glad to go to that place where, on their arrival, they may hope to obtain that which they longed for throughout life? But they longed for wisdom, and to be freed from association with that which they hated.

Have many of their own accord wished to descend into Hades, on account of human objects of affection, their wives and sons, induced by this very hope of their seeing and being with those whom they have loved? and shall one who really loves wisdom, and firmly cherishes this very hope, that he shall nowhere else attain it in a manner worthy of the name, except in Hades, be grieved at dying, and not gladly go there? We must think that he would gladly go, my friend, if he be in truth a philosopher; for he will be firmly persuaded of this, that he will nowhere else than there attain wisdom in its purity; and if this be so, would it not be very irrational, as I just now said, if such a man were to be afraid of death?"

"Very much so, by Jupiter!" he replied.

"Would not this, then," he resumed, "be a sufficient proof to you with respect to a man whom you should see grieved when about to die, that he was not a lover of wisdom, but a lover of his body? And this same person is probably a lover of riches and a lover of honor, one or both of these."

"It certainly is as you say," he replied.

"Does not, then," he said, "that which is called fortitude, Simmias, eminently belong to philosophers?"

"By all means," he answered.

"And temperance, also, which even the multitude call temperance, and which consists in not being carried away by the passions, but in holding them in contempt, and keeping them in subjection, does not this belong to those only who most despise the body, and live in the study of philosophy?"

"Necessarily so," he replied.

"For," he continued, "if you will consider the fortitude and temperance of others, they will appear to you to be absurd."

"How so, Socrates?"

"Do you know," he said, "that all others consider death among the great evils?"

"They do indeed," he answered.

"Then, do the brave among them endure death when they do endure it, through dread of greater evils?"

"It is so."

"All men, therefore, except philosophers, are brave through being afraid and fear; though it is absurd that anyone should be brave through fear and cowardice."

"Certainly."

"But what, are not those among them who keep their passions in subjection affected in the same way? and are they not temperate through a kind of intemperance? And although we may say, perhaps, that this is impossible, nevertheless the manner in which they are affected with respect to this silly temperance resembles this, for, fearing to be deprived of other pleasures, and desiring them, they abstain from some, being mastered by others. And though they call intemperance the being governed by pleasures, yet it happens to them that, by being mastered by some pleasures, they master others, and this is similar to what was just now said, that in a certain manner they become temperate through intemperance."

"So it seems,"

"My dear Simmias, consider that this is not a right exchange for virtue, to barter pleasures for pleasures, pains for pains, fear for fear, and the greater for the lesser, like pieces of money, but that that alone is the right coin, for which we ought to barter all these things, wisdom, and for this and with this everything is in reality bought and sold Fortitude, temperance and justice, and, in a word true virtue, subsist with wisdom, whether pleasures and fears, and everything else of the kind, are present or absent, but when separated from wisdom and changed one for another, consider whether such virtue is not a mere outline and in reality servile, possessing neither soundness nor truth. But the really true virtue is a purification from all such things, and temperance, justice, fortitude and wisdom itself, are a kind of initiatory purification 38. And those who instituted the mysteries for us appear to have been by no means contemptible, but in reality to have intimated long since that whoever shall arrive in Hades unexpiated and uninitiated shall lie in mud, but he that arrives there purified and initiated shall dwell with the gods 'For there are,' say those who preside at the mysteries, 'many wand-bearers, but few inspired'. These last, in my opinion, are no other than those who have pursued philosophy rightly that I might be of their number. I have to the utmost of my ability left no means untried, but have endeavored to the utmost of my power. But whether I have endeavored rightly, and have in any respect succeeded, on arriving there I shall know clearly, if it please God—very shortly, as it appears to me."

"Such, then, Simmias and Cebes," he added, "is the defense I make, for that I, on good grounds, do not repine or grieve at leaving you and my masters here, being persuaded that there, no less than here, I shall meet with good masters and friends. But to the multitude this is incredible If, however, I have succeeded better with you in my defense than I did with the Athenian judges, it is well."

When Socrates had thus spoken, Cebes, taking up the discussion, said "Socrates, all the rest appears to me to be said rightly, but what you have said respecting the soul will occasion much incredulity in many from the apprehension that when it is separated from the body it no longer exists anywhere, but is destroyed and perishes on the very day in which a man dies, and that immediately it is separated and goes out from the body it is dispersed, and vanishes like breath or smoke, and is no longer anywhere, since if it remained anywhere united in itself, and freed from those evils which you have just now enumerated, there would be an abundant and good hope, Socrates, that what you say is true 40. But this probably needs no little persuasion and proof, that the soul of a man who dies exists, and possesses activity and intelligence."

"You say truly, Cebes," said Socrates, "but what shall we do? Are you willing that we should converse on these points, whether such is probably the case or not?"

"Indeed," replied Cebes, "I should gladly hear your opinion on these matters."

"I do not think," said Socrates, "that anyone who should now hear us, even though he were a comic poet, would say that I am talking idly, or discoursing on subjects that do not concern me. If you please, then, we will examine into it. Let us consider it in this point of view, whether the souls of men who are dead exist in Hades, or not. This is an ancient saying, which we now call to mind, that souls departing hence exist there, and return hither again, and are produced from the dead. 41. And if this is so, that the living are produced again from the dead, can there be any other consequence than that our souls are there? for surely they could not be produced again if they did not exist; and this would be sufficient proof that these things are so, if it should in reality be evident that the living are produced from no other source than the dead. But if this is not the case, there will be need of other arguments."

"Certainly," said Cebes.

"You must not, then," he continued, "consider this only with respect to men, if you wish to ascertain it with greater certainty, but also with respect to all animals and plants, and, in a word, with respect to everything that is subject to generation. Let us see whether they are not all so produced, no otherwise than contraries from contraries, wherever they have any such quality; as, for instance, the honorable is contrary to the base, and the just to the unjust, and so with ten thousand other things. 42. Let us consider this, then, whether it is necessary that all things which have a contrary should be produced from nothing else than their contrary. As, for instance, when anything becomes greater, is it not necessary that, from being previously smaller, it afterward became greater?"

"Yes."

"And if it becomes smaller, will it not, from being previously greater, afterward become smaller?"

"It is so," he replied.

"And from stronger, weaker? and from slower, swifter?"

"Certainly."

"What, then? If anything becomes worse, must it not become so from better? and if more just, from more unjust?"

"How should it not?"

"We have then," he said, "sufficiently determined this, that all things are thus produced, contraries from contraries?"

"Certainly."

"What next? Is there also something of this kind in them; for instance, between all two contraries a mutual twofold production, from one to the other, and from that other back again? for between a greater thing and a smaller there are increase and decrease, and do we not accordingly call the one to increase, the other to decrease?"

"Yes," he replied.

"And must not to be separated and commingled, to grow cold and to grow warm, and everything in the same manner, even though sometimes we have not names to designate them, yet in fact be everywhere thus circumstanced, of necessity, as to be produced from each other, and be subject to a reciprocal generation?"

"Certainly," he replied.

"What, then?" said Socrates, "has life any contrary, as waking has its contrary, sleeping?"

"Certainly," he answered.

"What?"

"Death," he replied.

"Are not these, then, produced from each other, since they are contraries; and are not the modes by which they are produced two-fold intervening between these two?"

"How should it be otherwise?"

"I then," continued Socrates, "will describe to you one pair of the contraries which I have just now mentioned, both what it is and its mode of production: and do you describe to me the other. I say that one is to sleep, the other to awake; and from sleeping awaking is produced, and from awaking sleeping, and that the modes of their production are, the one to fall asleep, the other to be roused. 44. Have I sufficiently explained this to you or not?"

"Certainly."

"Do you, then," he said, "describe to me in the same manner with respect to life and death? Do you not say that life is contrary to death?"

"I do."

"And that they are produced from each other?"

"Yes."

"What, then, is produced from life?"

"Death," he replied.

"What, then," said he "is produced from death?"

"I must needs confess," he replied, "that life is."

"From the dead, then, O Cebes! living things and living men are produced."

"It appears so," he said.

"Our souls, therefore," said Socrates, "exist in Hades."

"So it seems."

"With respect, then, to their mode of production, is not one of them very clear? for to die surely is clear, is it not?"

"Certainly," he replied.

"What, then, shall we do?" he continued; "shall we not find a corresponding contrary mode of production, or will nature be defective in this? Or must we discover a contrary mode of production to dying?"

"By all means," he said.

"What is this?"

"To revive."

"Therefore," he proceeded, "if there is such a thing as to revive, will not this reviving be a mode of production from the dead to the living?"

"Certainly."

"Thus, then, we have agreed that the living are produced from the dead, no less than the dead from the living; but, this being the case, there appears to me sufficient proof that the souls of the dead must necessarily exist somewhere, from whence they are again produced."

"It appears to me, Socrates," he said "that this must necessarily follow from what has been admitted."

"See now, O Cebes!" he said, "that we have not agreed on these things improperly, as it appears to me; for if one class of things were not constantly given back in the place of another, revolving, as it were, in a circle, but generation were direct from one thing alone into its opposite, and did not turn round again to the other, or retrace its course, do you know that all things would at length have the same form, be in the same state, and cease to be produced?"

"How say you?" he asked.

"It is by no means difficult," he replied, "to understand what I mean; if, for instance, there should be such a thing as falling asleep, but no reciprocal waking again produced from a state of sleep, you know that at length all things would show the fable of Endymion to be a jest, and it would be thought nothing at all of, because everything else would be in the same state as he—namely, asleep. And if all things were mingled together, but never separated, that doctrine of Anaxagoras would soon be verified, 'all things would be together.' 46. Likewise, my dear Cebes, if all things that partake of life should die, and after they are dead should remain in this state of death, and not revive again, would it not necessarily follow that at length all things should be dead, and nothing alive? For if living beings are produced from other things, and living beings die, what could prevent their being all absorbed in death?"

"Nothing whatever, I think, Socrates," replied Cebes; "but you appear to me to speak the exact truth."

"For, Cebes," he continued, "as it seems to me, such undoubtedly is the case, and we have not admitted these things under a delusion, for it is in reality true that there is a reviving again, that the living are produced from the dead, that the souls of the dead exist, and that the condition of the good is better, and of the evil worse."

"And, indeed," said Cebes, interrupting him, "according to that doctrine, Socrates, which you are frequently in the habit of advancing, if it is true, that our learning is nothing else than reminiscence, according to this it is surely necessary that we must at some former time have learned what we now remember. But this is impossible, unless our soul existed somewhere before it came into this human form; so that from hence, also, the soul appears to be something immortal."

"But, Cebes," said Simmias, interrupting him, "what proofs are there of these things? Remind me of them, for I do not very well remember them at present."

"It is proved," said Cebes, "by one argument, and that a most beautiful one, that men, when questioned (if one questions them properly) of themselves, describe all things as they are, however, if they had not innate knowledge and right reason, they would never be able to do this. Moreover, if one leads them to diagrams, or anything else of the kind, it is then most clearly apparent that this is the case."

"But if you are not persuaded in this way, Simmias," said Socrates, "see if you will agree with us in considering the matter thus. For do you doubt how that which is called learning is reminiscence?"

"I do not doubt," said Simmias; "but I require this very thing of which we are speaking, to be reminded; and, indeed, from what Cebes has begun to say, I almost now remember, and am persuaded; nevertheless, however, I should like to hear now how you would attempt to prove it."

"I do it thus" he replied: "we admit, surely, that if anyone be reminded of anything, he must needs have known that thing at some time or other before."

"Certainly," he said.

"Do we, then, admit this also, that when knowledge comes in a certain manner it is reminiscence? But the manner I mean is this: if anyone, upon seeing or hearing, or perceiving through the medium of any other sense, some particular thing, should not only know that, but also form an idea of something else, of which the knowledge is not the same, but different, should we not justly say that he remembered that of which he received the idea?"

"How mean you?"

"For instance, the knowledge of a man is different from that of a lyre."

"How not?"

"Do you not know, then, that lovers when they see a lyre, or a garment, or anything else which their favorite is accustomed to use, are thus affected; they both recognize the lyre, and receive in their minds the form of the person to whom the lyre belonged? This is reminiscence: just as anyone, seeing Simmias, is often reminded of Cebes, and so in an infinite number of similar instances."

"An infinite number, indeed, by Jupiter!" said Simmias.

"Is not, then," he said, "something of this sort a kind of reminiscence, especially when one is thus affected with respect to things which, from lapse of time, and not thinking of them, one has now forgotten?"

"Certainly," he replied.

"But what?" he continued. "Does it happen that when one sees a painted horse or a painted lyre one is reminded of a man, and that when one sees a picture of Simmias one is reminded of Cebes?"

"Certainly."

"And does it not also happen that on seeing a picture of Simmias one is reminded of Simmias himself?"

"It does, indeed," he replied.

"Does it not happen, then, according to all this, that reminiscence arises partly from things like, and partly from things unlike?"

"It does."

"But when one is reminded by things like, is it not necessary that one should be thus further affected, so as to perceive whether, as regards likeness, this falls short or not of the thing of which one has been reminded?"

"It is necessary," he replied.

"Consider, then," said Socrates, "if the case is thus. Do we allow that there is such a thing as equality? I do not mean of one log with another, nor one stone with another, nor anything else of this kind, but something altogether different from all these—abstract equality; do we allow that there is any such thing, or not?"

"By Jupiter! we most assuredly do allow it," replied Simmias.

"And do we know what it is itself?"

"Certainly," he replied.

"Whence have we derived the knowledge of it? Is it not from the things we have just now mentioned, and that from seeing logs, or stones, or other things of the kind, equal, we have from these formed an idea of that which is different from these—for does it not appear to you to be different? Consider the matter thus. Do not stones that are equal, and logs sometimes that are the same, appear at one time equal, and at another not?"

"Certainly."

"But what? Does abstract equality ever appear to you unequal? or equality inequality?"

"Never, Socrates, at any time."

"These equal things, then," he said, "and abstract equality, are not the same?"

"By no means, Socrates, as it appears."

"However, from these equal things," he said, "which are different from that abstract equality, have you not formed your idea and derived your knowledge of it?"

"You speak most truly," he replied.

"Is it not, therefore, from its being like or unlike them?"

"Certainly."

"But it makes no difference," he said. "When, therefore, on seeing one thing, you form, from the sight of it, the notion of another, whether like or unlike, this," he said, "must necessarily be reminiscence."

"Certainly."

"What, then, as to this?" he continued. "Are we affected in any such way with regard to logs and the equal things we have just now spoken of? And do they appear to us to be equal in the same manner as abstract equality itself is, or do they fall short in some degree, or not at all, of being such as equality itself is?"

"They fall far short," he replied.

"Do we admit, then, that when one, on beholding some particular thing, perceives that it aims, as that which I now see, at being like something else that exists, but falls short of it, and cannot become such as that is, but is inferior to it—do we admit that he who perceives this must necessarily have had a previous knowledge of that which he says it resembles, though imperfectly?"

"It is necessary."

"What, then? Are we affected in some such way, or not, with respect to things equal and abstract equality itself?"

"Assuredly."

"It is necessary, therefore, that we must have known abstract equality before the time when, on first seeing equal things, we perceived that they all aimed at resembling equality, but failed in doing so."

"Such is the case."

"Moreover, we admit this too, that we perceived this, and could not possibly perceive it by any other means than the sight, or touch, or some other of the senses, for I say the same of them all."

"For they are the same, Socrates, so far as, our argument is concerned."

"However, we must perceive, by means of the senses, that all things which come under the senses aim at that abstract equality, and yet fall short of it; or how shall we say it is?"

"Even so."

"Before, then, we began to see, and hear, and use our other senses, we must have had a knowledge of equality itself—what it is, if we were to refer to it those equal things that come under the senses, and observe that all such things aim at resembling that, but fall far short of it."

"This necessarily follows, Socrates, from what has been already said."

"But did we not, as soon as we were born, see and hear, and possess our other senses?"

"Certainly."

"But, we have said, before we possessed these, we must have had a knowledge of abstract equality?"

"Yes."

"We must have had it, then, as it seems, before we were born."

"It seems so."

"If, therefore, having this before we were born, we were born possessing it, we knew, both before we were born and as soon as we were born, not only the equal and the greater and smaller, but all things of the kind; for our present discussion is not more respecting equality than the beautiful itself, the good, the just, and the holy, and, in one word, respecting everything which we mark with the seal of existence, both in the questions we ask and the answers we give. So that we must necessarily have had a knowledge of all these before we were born."

"Such is the case."

"And if, having once had it, we did not constantly forget it, we should always be born with this knowledge, and should always retain it through life. For to know is this, when one has got a knowledge of anything, to retain and not lose it; for do we not call this oblivion, Simmias, the loss of knowledge?"

"Assuredly, Socrates," he replied.

"But if, having had it before we were born, we lose it at our birth, and afterward, through exercising the senses about these things, we recover the knowledge which we once before possessed, would not that which we call learning be a recovery of our own knowledge? And in saying that this is to remember, should we not say rightly?"

"Certainly."

"For this appeared to be possible, for one having perceived anything, either by seeing or hearing, or employing any other sense, to form an idea of something different from this, which he had forgotten, and with which this was connected by being unlike or like. So that, as I said, one of these two things must follow: either we are all born with this knowledge, and we retain it through life, or those whom we say learn afterward do nothing else than remember, and this learning will be reminiscence."

"Such, certainly, is the case, Socrates."

"Which, then, do you choose, Simmias: that we are born with knowledge, or that we afterward remember what we had formerly known?"

"At present, Socrates, I am unable to choose."

"But what? Are you able to choose in this case, and what do you think about it? Can a man who possesses knowledge give a reason for the things that he knows, or not?"

"He needs must be able to do so, Socrates," he replied.

"And do all men appear to you to be able to give a reason for the things of which we have just now been speaking?"

"I wish they could," said Simmias; "but I am much more afraid that at this time to-morrow there will no longer be anyone able to do this properly."

"Do not all men, then, Simmias," he said, "seem to you to know these things?"

"By no means."

"Do they remember, then, what they once learned?"

"Necessarily so."

"When did our souls receive this knowledge? Not surely, since we were born into the world."

"Assuredly not."

"Before, then?"

"Yes."

"Our souls, therefore, Simmias, existed before they were in a human form, separate from bodies, and possessed intelligence."

"Unless, Socrates, we receive this knowledge at our birth, for this period yet remains."

"Be it so, my friend. But at what other time do we lose it? for we are not born with it, as we have just now admitted. Do we lose it, then, at the very time in which we receive it? Or can you mention any other time?"

"By no means, Socrates; I was not aware that I was saying nothing to the purpose."

"Does the case then stand thus with us, Simmias?" he proceeded: "If those things which we are continually talking about really exist, the beautiful, the good, and every such essence, and to this we refer all things that come under the senses, as finding it to have a prior existence, and to be our own, and if we compare these things to it, it necessarily follows, that as these exist, so likewise our soul exists even before we are born; but if these do not exist, this discussion will have been undertaken in vain, is it not so? And is there not an equal necessity both that these things should exist, and our souls also, before we are born; and if not the former, neither the latter?"

"Most assuredly, Socrates," said Simmias, "there appears to me to be the same necessity; and the argument admirably tends to prove that our souls exist before we are born, just as that essence does which you have now mentioned. For I hold nothing so clear to me as this, that all such things most certainly exist, as the beautiful, the good, and all the rest that you just now spoke of; and, so far as I am concerned, the case is sufficiently demonstrated."

"But how does it appear to Cebes?" said Socrates; "for it is necessary to persuade Cebes too."

"He is sufficiently persuaded, I think," said Simmias, "although he is the most pertinacious of men in distrusting arguments. Yet I think he is sufficiently persuaded of this, that our soul existed before we were born. But whether, when we are dead, it will still exist does not appear to me to have been demonstrated, Socrates," he continued; "but that popular doubt, which Cebes just now mentioned, still stands in our way, whether, when a man dies, the soul is not dispersed, and this is the end of its existence. For what hinders it being born, and formed from some other source, and existing before it came into a human body, and yet, when it has come, and is separated from this body, its then also dying itself, and being destroyed?"

"You say well, Simmias," said Cebes; "for it appears that only one half of what is necessary has been demonstrated—namely, that our soul existed before we were born; but it is necessary to demonstrate further, that when we are dead it will exist no less than before we were born, if the demonstration is to be made complete."

"This has been even now demonstrated, Simmias and Cebes," said Socrates, "if you will only connect this last argument with that which we before assented to, that everything living is produced from that which is dead. For if the soul exists before, and it is necessary for it when it enters into life, and is born, to be produced from nothing else than death, and from being dead, how is it not necessary for it also to exist after death, since it must needs be produced again? What you require, then, has been already demonstrated. However, both you and Simmias appear to me as if you wished to sift this argument more thoroughly, and to be afraid, like children, lest, on the soul's departure from the body, the winds should blow it away and disperse it, especially if one should happen to die, not in a calm, but in a violent storm."

Upon this Cebes, smiling, said, "Endeavor to teach us better, Socrates, as if we were afraid, or rather not as if we were afraid, though perhaps there is some boy[30] within us who has such a dread. Let us, then, endeavor to persuade him not to be afraid of death, as of hobgoblins."

"But you must charm him every day," said Socrates, "until you have quieted his fears."

"But whence, Socrates," he said, "can we procure a skillful charmer for such a case, now that you are about to leave us?"

"Greece is wide, Cebes," he replied, "and in it surely there are skillful men. There are also many barbarous nations, all of which you should search through, seeking such a charmer, sparing neither money nor toil, as there is nothing on which you can more seasonably spend your money. You should also seek for him among yourselves; for perhaps you could not easily find any more competent than yourselves to do this."

"This shall be done," said Cebes; "but, if it is agreeable to you, let us return to the point from whence we digressed."

"It will be agreeable to me, for how should it not?"

"You say well," rejoined Cebes.

"We ought, then," said Socrates, "to ask ourselves some such question as this: to what kind of thing it appertains to be thus affected—namely, to be dispersed—and for what we ought to fear, lest it should be so affected, and for what not. And after this we should consider which of the two the soul is, and in the result should either be confident or fearful for our soul."

"You speak truly," said he.

"Does it not, then, appertain to that which is formed by composition, and is naturally compounded, to be thus affected, to be dissolved in the same manner as that in which it was compounded; and if there is anything not compounded, does it not appertain to this alone, if to anything, not to be thus affected?"

"It appears to me to be so," said Cebes.

"Is it not most probable, then, that things which are always the same, and in the same state, are uncompounded, but that things which are constantly changing, and are never in the same state, are compounded?"

"To me it appears so."

"Let us return, then," he said, "to the subjects on which we before discoursed. Whether is essence itself, of which we gave this account that it exists, both in our questions and answers, always the same, or does it sometimes change? Does equality itself, the beautiful itself, and each several thing which is, ever undergo any change, however small? Or does each of them which exists, being an unmixed essence by itself, continue always the same, and in the same state, and never undergo any variation at all under any circumstances?"

"They must of necessity continue the same and in the same state, Socrates," said Cebes.

"But what shall we say of the many beautiful things, such as men, horses, garments, or other things of the kind, whether equal or beautiful, or of all things synonymous with them? Do they continue the same, or, quite contrary to the former, are they never at any time, so to say, the same, either with respect to themselves or one another?"

"These, on the other hand," replied Cebes, "never continue the same."

"These, then, you can touch, or see, or perceive by the other senses; but those that continue the same, you cannot apprehend in any other way than by the exercise of thought; for such things are invisible, and are not seen?"

"You say what is strictly true," replied Cebes.

"We may assume, then, if you please," he continued, "that there are two species of things; the one visible, the other invisible?"

"We may," he said.

"And the invisible always continuing the same, but the visible never the same?"

"This, too," he said, "we may assume."

"Come, then," he asked, "is there anything else belonging to us than, on the one hand, body, and, on the other, soul?"

"Nothing else," he replied.

"To which species, then, shall we say the body is more like, and more nearly allied?"

"It is clear to everyone," he said, "that it is to the visible."

"But what of the soul? Is it visible or invisible?"

"It is not visible to men, Socrates," he replied.

"But we speak of things which are visible, or not so, to the nature of men; or to some other nature, think you?"

"To that of men."

"What, then, shall we say of the soul—that it is visible, or not visible?"

"Not visible."

"Is it, then, invisible?"

"Yes."

"The soul, then, is more like the invisible than the body; and the body, the visible?"

"It must needs be so, Socrates."

"And did we not, some time since, say this too, that the soul, when it employs the body to examine anything, either by means of the sight or hearing, or any other sense (for to examine anything by means of the body is to do so by the senses), is then drawn by the body to things that never continue the same, and wanders and is confused, and reels as if intoxicated, through coming into contact with things of this kind?"

"Certainly."

"But when it examines anything by itself, does it approach that which is pure, eternal, immortal, and unchangeable, and, as being allied to it, continue constantly with it, so long as it subsists by itself, and has the power, and does it cease from its wandering, and constantly continue the same with respect to those things, through coming into contact with things of this kind? And is this affection of the soul called wisdom?"

"You speak," he said, "in every respect, well and truly, Socrates."

"To which species of the two, then, both from what was before and now said, does the soul appear to you to be more like and more nearly allied?"

"Everyone, I think, would allow, Socrates," he replied, "even the dullest person, from this method of reasoning, that the soul is in every respect more like that which continues constantly the same than that which does not so."

"But what as to the body?"

"It is more like the other."

"Consider it also thus, that, when soul and body are together, nature enjoins the latter to be subservient and obey, the former to rule and exercise dominion. And, in this way, which of the two appears to you to be like the divine, and which the mortal? Does it not appear to you to be natural that the divine should rule and command, but the mortal obey and be subservient?"

"To me it does so."

"Which, then, does the soul resemble?"

"It is clear, Socrates, that the soul resembles the divine; but the body, the mortal."

"Consider, then, Cebes," said he, "whether, from all that has been said, these conclusions follow, that the soul is most like that which is divine, immortal, intelligent, uniform, indissoluble, and which always continues in the same state; but that the body, on the other hand, is most like that which is human, mortal, unintelligent, multiform, dissoluble, and which never continues in the same state. Can we say anything against this, my dear Cebes, to show that it is not so?"

"We cannot."

"What, then? Since these things are so, does it not appertain to the body to be quickly dissolved, but to the soul, on the contrary, to be altogether indissoluble or nearly so?"

"How not?"

"You perceive, however," he said, "that when a man dies, the visible part of him, the body, which is exposed to sight, and which we call a corpse, to which it appertains to be dissolved, to fall asunder and be dispersed, does not immediately undergo any of these affections, but remains for a considerable time, and especially so if anyone should die with his body in full vigor, and at a corresponding age;[31] for when the body has collapsed and been embalmed, as those that are embalmed in Egypt, it remains almost entire for an incredible length of time; and some parts of the body, even though it does decay, such as the bones and nerves, and everything of that kind, are, nevertheless, as one may say, immortal. Is it not so?"

"Yes."

"Can the soul, then, which is invisible, and which goes to another place like itself, excellent, pure and invisible, and therefore truly called the invisible world,[32] to the presence of a good and wise God (whither, if God will, my soul also must shortly go)—can this soul of ours, I ask, being such and of such a nature, when separated from the body, be immediately dispersed and destroyed, as most men assert? Far from it, my dear Cebes and Simmias. But the case is much rather thus: if it is separated in a pure state, taking nothing of the body with it, as not having willingly communicated with it in the present life, but having shunned it, and gathered itself within itself, as constantly studying this (but this is nothing else than to pursue philosophy aright, and in reality to study how to die easily), would not this be to study how to die?"

"Most assuredly."

"Does not the soul, then, when in this state, depart to that which resembles itself, the invisible, the divine, immortal and wise? And on its arrival there, is it not its lot to be happy, free from error, ignorance, fears, wild passions, and all the other evils to which human nature is subject; and, as is said of the initiated, does it not in truth pass the rest of its time with the gods? Must we affirm that it is so, Cebes, or otherwise?"

"So, by Jupiter!" said Cebes.

"But, I think, if it departs from the body polluted and impure, as having constantly held communion with the body, and having served and loved it, and been bewitched by it, through desires and pleasures, so as to think that there is nothing real except what is corporeal, which one can touch and see, and drink and eat, and employ for sensual purposes; but what is dark and invisible to the eyes, which is intellectual and apprehended by philosophy, having been accustomed to hate, fear, and shun this, do you think that a soul thus affected can depart from the body by itself, and uncontaminated?"

"By no means whatever," he replied.

"But I think it will be impressed with that which is corporeal, which the intercourse and communion of the body, through constant association and great attention, have made natural to it."

"Certainly."

"We must think, my dear Cebes, that this is ponderous and heavy, earthly and visible, by possessing which such a soul is weighed down, and drawn again into the visible world through dread of the invisible and of Hades, wandering, as it is said, among monuments and tombs, about which, indeed, certain shadowy phantoms of souls have been seen, being such images as those souls produced which have not departed pure from the body, but which partake of the visible; on which account, also, they are visible."

"That is probable, Socrates."

"Probable indeed, Cebes; and not that these are the souls of the good, but of the wicked, which are compelled to wander about such places, paying the penalty of their former conduct, which was evil; and they wander about so long until, through the desire of the corporeal nature that accompanies them, they are again united to a body; and they are united, as is probable, to animals having the same habits as those they have given themselves up to during life."

"But what do you say these are, Socrates?"

"For instance, those who have given themselves up to gluttony, wantonness and drinking, and have put no restraint on themselves, will probably be clothed in the form of asses and brutes of that kind. Do you not think so?"

"You say what is very probable."

"And that such as have set great value on injustice, tyranny and rapine, will be clothed in the species of wolves, hawks and kites! Where else can we say such souls go?"

"Without doubt," said Cebes, "into such as these."

"Is it not, then, evident," he continued, "as to the rest, whither each will go, according to the resemblances of their several pursuits?"

"It is evident," he replied. "How not?"

"Of these, then," he said, "are not they the most happy, and do they not go to the best place, who have practiced that social and civilized virtue which they call temperance and justice, and which is produced from habit and exercise, without philosophy and reflection?"

"In what respect are these the most happy?"

"Because it is probable that these should again migrate into a corresponding civilized and peaceable kind of animals, such as bees perhaps, or wasps, or ants, or even into the same human species again, and from these become moderate men."

74

"It is probable."

"But it is not lawful for anyone who has not studied philosophy, and departed this life perfectly pure, to pass into the rank of gods, but only for the true lover of wisdom. And on this account, my friends Simmias and Cebes, those who philosophize rightly, abstain from all bodily desires, and persevere in doing so, and do not give themselves up to them, not fearing the loss of property and poverty, as the generality of men and the lovers of wealth; nor, again, dreading disgrace and ignominy, like those who are lovers of power and honor, do they then abstain from them."

"For it would not become them to do so, Socrates," says Cebes.

"It would not, by Jupiter!" he rejoined. "Wherefore, Cebes, they who care at all for their soul, and do not spend their lives in the culture of their bodies, despising all these, proceed not in the same way with them, as being ignorant whither they are going, but, being convinced that they ought not to act contrary to philosophy, but in accordance with the freedom and purification she affords, they give themselves up to her direction, following her wherever she leads."

"How, Socrates?"

"I will tell you," he replied. "The lovers of wisdom know that philosophy, receiving their soul plainly bound and glued to the body, and compelled to view things through this, as through a prison, and not directly by herself, and sunk in utter ignorance, and perceiving, too, the strength of the prison, that it arises from desire, so that he who is bound as much as possible assists in binding himself. 73. I say, then, the lovers of wisdom know that philosophy, receiving their soul in this state, gently exhorts it, and endeavors to free it, by showing that the view of things by means of the eyes is full of deception, as also is that through the ears and the other senses; persuading an abandonment of these so far as it is not absolutely necessary to use them, and advising the soul to be collected and concentrated within itself, and to believe nothing else than herself, with respect to what she herself understands of things that have a real subsistence; and to consider nothing true which she views through the medium of others, and which differ under different aspects;[32] for that a thing of this kind is sensible and visible, but that what she herself perceives is intelligible and invisible. The soul of the true philosopher, therefore, thinking that she ought not to oppose this deliverance, accordingly abstains as much as possible from pleasures and desires, griefs and fears, considering that when anyone is exceedingly delighted or alarmed, grieved or influenced by desire, he does not merely suffer such evil from these things as one might suppose, such as either being sick or wasting his property through indulging his desires; but that which is the greatest evil, and the worst of all, this he suffers, and is not conscious of it."

"But what is this evil, Socrates?" said Cebes.

"That the soul of every man is compelled to be either vehemently delighted or grieved about some particular thing, and, at the same time, to consider that the thing about which it is thus strongly affected is most real and most true, though it is not so. But these are chiefly visible objects, are they not?"

"Certainly."

"In this state of affection, then, is not the soul especially shackled by the body?"

"How so?"

"Because each pleasure and pain, having a nail, as it were, nails the soul to the body, and fastens it to it, and causes it to become corporeal, deeming those things to be true whatever the body asserts to be so. For, in consequence of its forming the same opinions with the body, and delighting in the same things, it is compelled, I think, to possess similar manners, and to be similarly nourished; so that it can never pass into Hades in a pure state, but must ever depart polluted by the body, and so quickly falls again into another body, and grows up as if it were sown, and consequently is deprived of all association with that which is divine, and pure, and uniform."

"You speak most truly, Socrates," said Cebes.

"For these reasons, therefore, Cebes, those who are truly lovers of wisdom are moderate and resolute, and not for the reasons that most people say. Do you think as they do?"

"Assuredly not."

"No, truly. But the soul of a philosopher would reason thus, and would not think that philosophy ought to set it free, and that when it is freed it should give itself up again to pleasures and pains, to bind it down again, and make her work void, weaving a kind of Penelope's web the reverse way. On the contrary, effecting a calm of the passions, and following the guidance of reason, and being always intent on this, contemplating that which is true and divine, and not subject to opinion; and being nourished by it, it thinks that it ought to live in this manner as long as it does live, and that when it dies it shall go to a kindred essence, and one like itself, and shall be free from human evils. From such a regimen as this the soul has no occasion to fear, Simmias and Cebes, while it strictly attends to these things, lest, being torn to pieces at its departure from the body, it should be blown about and dissipated by the winds, and no longer have an existence anywhere."

When Socrates had thus spoken, a long silence ensued; and Socrates himself was pondering upon what had been said, as he appeared, and so did most of us; but Cebes and Simmias were conversing a little while with each other. At length

Socrates, perceiving them, said, "What think you of what has been said? Does it appear to you to have been proved sufficiently? for many doubts and objections still remain if anyone will examine them thoroughly. If, then, you are considering some other subject, I have nothing to say; but if you are doubting about this, do not hesitate both yourselves to speak and express your opinion, if it appears to you in any respect that it might have been argued better, and to call me in again to your assistance, if you think you can be at all benefited by my help."

Upon this Simmias said, "Indeed, Socrates, I will tell you the truth: for some time each of us, being in doubt, has been urging and exhorting the other to question you, from a desire to hear our doubts solved; but we were afraid of giving you trouble, lest it should be disagreeable to you in your present circumstances."

But he, upon hearing this, gently smiled, and said, "Bless me, Simmias; with difficulty, indeed, could I persuade other men that I do not consider my present condition a calamity, since I am not able to persuade even you; but you are afraid lest I should be more morose now than during the former part of my life. And, as it seems, I appear to you to be inferior to swans with respect to divination, who, when they perceive that they must needs die, though they have been used to sing before, sing then more than ever, rejoicing that they are about to depart to that deity whose servants they are. But men, through their own fear of death, belie the swans too, and say that they, lamenting their death, sing their last song through grief; and they do not consider that no bird sings when it is hungry or cold, or is afflicted with any other pain, not even the nightingale, or swallow, or the hoopoes, which, they say, sing lamenting through grief. But neither do these birds appear to me to sing through sorrow, nor yet do swans; but, in my opinion, belonging to Apollo, they are prophetic, and, foreseeing the blessings of Hades, they sing and rejoice on that day more excellently than at any preceding time.

But I, too, consider myself to be a fellow-servant of the swans, and sacred to the same god; and that I have received the power of divination from our common master no less than they, and that I do not depart from this life with less spirits than they. On this account, therefore, it is right that you should both speak and ask whatever you please, so long as the Athenian Eleven permit."

"You say well," said Simmias, "and both I will tell you what are my doubts, and he, in turn, how far he does not assent to what has been said. For it appears to me, Socrates, probably as it does to you with respect to these matters, that to know them clearly in the present life is either impossible or very difficult: on the other hand, however, not to test what has been said of them in every possible way, so as not to desist until, on examining them in every point of view, one has exhausted every effort, is the part of a very weak man. For we ought, with respect to these things, either to learn from others how they stand or to discover them for one's self; or, if both these are impossible, then, taking the best of human reasonings and that which is the most difficult to be confuted, and embarking on this, as one who risks himself on a raft, so to sail through life, unless one could be carried more safely, and with less risk, on a surer conveyance, or some divine reason.

I, therefore, shall not now be ashamed to question you, since you bid me do so, nor shall I blame myself hereafter for not having now told you what I think; for to me, Socrates, when I consider the matter, both with myself and with Cebes, what has been said does not appear to have been sufficiently proved."

Then said Socrates, "Perhaps, my friend, you have the truth on your side; but tell me in what respect it was not sufficiently proved."

"In this," he answered, "because anyone might use the same argument with respect to harmony, and a lyre, and its chords, that harmony is something invisible and incorporeal, very beautiful and divine, in a well-modulated lyre; but the lyre and its chords are bodies, and of corporeal form, compounded and earthly, and akin to that which is mortal. When anyone, then, has either broken the lyre, or cut or burst the chords, he might maintain from the same reasoning as yours that it is necessary the harmony should still exist and not be destroyed; for there could be no possibility that the lyre should subsist any longer when the chords are burst; and that the chords, which are of a mortal nature, should subsist, but that the harmony, which is of the same nature and akin to that which is divine and immortal, should become extinct, and perish before that which is mortal; but he might say that the harmony must needs subsist somewhere, and that the wood and chords must decay before it can undergo any change.

For I think, Socrates, that you yourself have arrived at this conclusion, that we consider the soul to be pretty much of this kind—namely, that our body being compacted and held together by heat and cold, dryness and moisture, and other such qualities, our soul is the fusion and harmony of these, when they are well and duly combined with each other. If, then, the soul is a kind of harmony, it is evident that when our bodies are unduly relaxed or strained, through diseases and other maladies, the soul must, of necessity, immediately perish, although it is most divine, just as other harmonies which subsist in sounds or in the various works of artisans; but that the remains of the body of each person last for a long time, till they are either burned or decayed. Consider, then, what we shall say to this reasoning, if anyone should maintain that the soul, being a fusion of the several qualities in the body, perishes first in that which is called death."

Socrates, therefore, looking steadfastly at us, as he was generally accustomed to do, and smiling, said, "Simmias indeed speaks justly. If, then, anyone of you is more prompt than I am, why does he not answer, for he seems to have handled my argument not badly? It appears to me, however, that before we make our reply we should first hear from Cebes, what he, too, objects to our argument, in order that, sometime intervening, we may consider what we shall say, and then when we have heard them, we may give up to them, if they appear to speak agreeably to truth; or, if not, we may then uphold our own argument. Come, then, Cebes," he continued, "say what it is that disturbs you, so as to cause your unbelief."

"I will tell you," said Cebes; "the argument seems to me to rest where it was, and to be liable to the same objection that we mentioned before. For, that our soul existed even before It came into this present form, I do not deny has been very elegantly, and, if it is not too much to say so, very fully, demonstrated; but that it still exists anywhere when we are dead does not appear to me to have been clearly proved; nor do I give in to the objection of Simmias, that the soul is not stronger and more durable than the body, for it appears to me to excel very far all things of this kind. 82. 'Why, then,' reason might say, 'do you still disbelieve? for, since you see that when a man dies his weaker part still exists, does it not appear to you to be necessary that the more durable part should still be preserved during this period?' Consider, then, whether I say anything to the purpose in reply to this. For I, too, as well as Simmias, as it seems, stand in need of an illustration; for the argument appears to me to have been put thus, as if anyone should advance this argument about an aged weaver who had died, that the man has not yet perished, but perhaps still exists somewhere; and, as a proof, should exhibit the garment which he wore and had woven himself, that it is entire and has not perished; and if anyone should disbelieve him, he would ask, which of the two is the more durable, the species of a man or of a garment, that is constantly in use and being worn; then, should anyone answer that the species of man is much more durable, he would think it demonstrated that, beyond all question, the man is preserved, since that which is less durable has not perished. 83. But I do not think, Simmias, that this is the case, and do you consider what I say, for everyone must think that he who argues thus argues, foolishly. For this weaver, having worn and woven many such garments, perished after almost all of them, but before the last, I suppose; and yet it does not on this account follow any the more that a man is inferior to or weaker than a garment. And I think, the soul might admit this same illustration with respect to the body, and he who should say the same things concerning them would appear to me to speak correctly, that the soul is more durable, but the body weaker and less durable; for he would say that each soul wears out many bodies, especially if it lives many years; for if the body wastes and is dissolved while the man still lives, but the soul continually weaves anew what is worn out, it must necessarily follow that when the soul is dissolved it must then have on its last garment, and perish before this alone; but when the soul has perished the body would show the weakness of its nature, and quickly rot and vanish. 84. So that it is not by any means right to place implicit reliance on this argument, and to believe that when we die our soul still exists somewhere. For, if anyone should concede to him who admits even more than you do, and should grant to him that not only did our soul exist before we were born, but that even when we die nothing hinders the souls of some of us from still existing, and continuing to exist hereafter, and from being often born, and dying again—for so strong is it by nature, that it can hold out against repeated births—if he granted this, he would not yet concede that it does not exhaust itself in its many births, and at length perish altogether in someone of the deaths. But he would say that no one knows this death and dissolution of the body, which brings destruction to the soul; for it is impossible for anyone of us to perceive it. If, however, this be the case, it follows that everyone who is confident at the approach of death is foolishly confident, unless he is able to prove that the soul is absolutely immortal and imperishable; otherwise it necessarily follows that he who is about to die must be alarmed for his soul, lest in its present disunion from the body it should entirely perish."

Upon this, all of us who had heard them speaking were disagreeably affected, as we afterward mentioned to each other; because, after we had been fully persuaded by the former arguments, they seemed to disturb us anew, and to cast us into a distrust, not only of the arguments already adduced, but of such as might afterward be urged, for fear lest we should not be fit judges of anything, or lest the things themselves should be incredible.

Echec. By the gods! Phædo, I can readily excuse you; for, while I am now hearing you, it occurs to me to ask myself some such question as this: What arguments can we any longer believe? since the argument which Socrates advanced, and which was exceedingly credible, has now fallen into discredit. For this argument, that our soul is a kind of harmony, produces a wonderful impression on me, both now and always, and in being mentioned, it has reminded me, as it were, that I, too, was formerly of the same opinion; so that I stand in need again, as if from the very beginning, of some other argument which may persuade me that the soul of one who dies does not die with the body. Tell me, therefore, by Jupiter! how Socrates followed up the argument; and whether he, too, as you confess was the case with yourselves, seemed disconcerted at all, or not, but calmly maintained his position; and maintained it sufficiently or defectively. Relate everything to me as accurately as you can.

Phaedo. Indeed, Echecrates, though I have often admired Socrates, I was never more delighted than at being with him on that occasion. That he should be able to say something is perhaps not at all surprising; but I especially admired this in him—first of all, that he listened to the argument of the young men so sweetly, affably, and approvingly; in the next place, that he so quickly perceived how we were affected by their arguments; and, lastly, that he cured us so well and recalled us, when we were put to flight, as it were, and vanquished, and encouraged us to accompany him, and consider the argument with him.

Echec. How was that?

Phaedo. I will tell you: I happened to be sitting at his right hand, near the bed, upon a low seat, but he himself sat much higher than I. Stroking my head, then, and laying hold of the hair that hung on my neck—for he used, often, to play with my hairs—"To-morrow," he said, "perhaps, Phædo, you will cut off these beautiful locks?"

"It seems likely, Socrates," said I.

"Not if you are persuaded by me."

"Why so?" I asked.

"To-day," he replied, "both I ought to cut off mine and you yours, if our argument must die, and we are unable to revive it. And I, if I were you, and the arguments were to escape me, would take an oath, as the Argives do, not to suffer my hair to grow until I had renewed the contest, and vanquished the arguments of Simmias and Cebes."

"But," I said, "even Hercules himself is said not to have been a match for two."

"Call upon me, then," he said, "as your Iolaus, while it is yet day."

"I do call on you, then," I said, "not as Hercules upon Iolaus, but as Iolaus upon Hercules."

"It will make no difference," he replied. "But, first of all, we must beware lest we meet with some mischance."

"What?" I asked.

"That we do not become," he answered, "haters of reasoning, as some become haters of men; for no greater evil can happen to anyone than to hate reasoning. But hatred of reasoning and hatred of mankind both spring from the same source. For hatred of mankind is produced in us from having placed too great reliance on someone without sufficient knowledge of him, and from having considered him to be a man altogether true, sincere, and faithful, and then, after a little while, finding him depraved and unfaithful, and after him another. And when a man has often experienced this, and especially from those whom he considered his most intimate and best friends, at length, having frequently stumbled, he hates all men, and thinks that there is no soundness at all in any of them. Have you not perceived that this happens so?"

"Certainly," I replied.

"Is it not a shame?" he said "And is it not evident that such a one attempts to deal with men without sufficient knowledge of human affairs? For if he had dealt with them with competent knowledge, as the case really is, so he would have considered that the good and the bad are each very few in number, and that those between both are most numerous."

"How say you?" I asked.

"In the same manner," he replied, "as with things very little and very large Do you think that anything is more rare than to find a very large on a very little man, or dog, or anything else? and, again, swift or slow, beautiful or ugly, white or black? Do you not perceive that of all such things the extremes are rare and few, but that the intermediate are abundant and numerous?"

"Certainly," I replied.

"Do you not think, then," he continued, "that if a contest in wickedness were proposed, even here very few would be found pre-eminent?"

"It is probable," I said.

"It is so," he said, "but in this respect reasonings do not resemble men, for I was just now following you as my leader, but in this they do resemble them, when anyone believes in any argument as true without being skilled in the art of reasoning, and then shortly afterward it appears to him to be false, at one time being so and at another time not, and so on with one after another,[34] and especially they who devote themselves to controversial arguments, you are aware, at length think they have become very wise and have alone discovered that there is nothing sound and stable either in things or reasonings but that all things that exist, as is the case with the Euripus, are in a constant state of flux and reflux, and never continue in anyone condition for any length of time."

"You speak perfectly true," I said.

"Would it not, then, Phædo" he said "be a sad thing if, when there is a true and sound reasoning, and such as one can understand, one should then, through lighting upon such arguments as appear to be at one time true and at another false, not blame one's self and one's own want of skill, but at length, through grief, should anxiously transfer the blame from one's self to the arguments, and thereupon pass the rest of one's life in hating and reviling arguments and so be depraved of the truth and knowledge of things that exist?"

"By Jupiter!" I said, "it would be sad, indeed."

"In the first place, then," he said, "let us beware of this, and let us not admit into our souls the notion that there appears to be nothing sound in reasoning, but much rather that we are not yet in a sound condition, and that we ought vigorously and strenuously to endeavor to become sound, you and the others, on account of your whole future life, but I, on account of my death, since I am in danger, at the present time, of not behaving as becomes a philosopher with respect to this very subject, but as a wrangler, like those who are utterly uninformed. For they, when they dispute about anything, care nothing at all for the subject about which the discussion is, but are anxious about this, that what they have themselves advanced shall appear true to the persons present. And I seem to myself on the present occasion to differ from them only in this respect, for I shall not be anxious to make what I say appear true to those who are present, except that may happen by the way, but that it may appear certainly to be so to myself. For I thus reason, my dear friend, and observe how interestedly. If what I say be true, it is well to be persuaded of it, but if nothing remains to one that is dead, I shall, at least, during the interval before death be less disagreeable to those present by my lamentations. But this ignorance of mine will not continue long, for that would be bad, but will shortly be put an end to. Thus prepared, then, Simmias and Cebes," he continued, "I now proceed to my argument. Do you, however, if you will be persuaded by me, pay little attention to Socrates, but much more to the truth, and if I appear to you to say anything true, assent to it, but if not, oppose me with all your might, taking good care that in my zeal I do not deceive both myself and you, and, like a bee, depart leaving my sting behind."

"But let us proceed," he said "First of all, remind me of what you said, if I should appear to have forgotten it For Simmias, as I think, is in doubt, and fears lest the soul, though more divine and beautiful than the body, should perish before it, as being a species of harmony. But Cebes appeared to me to grant me this, that the soul is more durable than the body, but he argued that it is uncertain to everyone, whether when the soul has worn out many bodies and that repeatedly, it does not, on leaving the last body, itself also perish, so that this very thing is death, the destruction of the soul, since the body never ceases decaying Are not these the things, Simmias and Cebes, which we have to inquire into?"

They both agreed that they were.

"Whether, then," he continued "do you reject all our former arguments, or some of them only, and not others?"

"Some we do," they replied, "and others not."

"What, then," he proceeded, "do you say about that argument in which we asserted that knowledge is reminiscence, and that, this being the case, our soul must necessarily have existed somewhere before it was inclosed in the body?"

"I, indeed," replied Cebes "was both then wonderfully persuaded by it, and now persist in it, as in no other argument."

"And I, too," said Simmias, "am of the same mind, and should very much wonder if I should ever think otherwise on that point."

"Then," Socrates said, "you must needs think otherwise, my Theban friend, if this opinion holds good, that harmony is something compounded, and that the soul is a kind of harmony that results from the parts compacted together in the body. For surely you will not allow yourself to say that harmony was composed prior to the things from which it required to be composed Would you allow this?"

"By no means, Socrates" he replied.

"Do you perceive, then," he said, "that this result from what you say, when you assert that the soul existed before it came into a human form and body, but that it was composed from things that did not yet exist? For harmony is not such as that to which you compare it, but first the lyre, and the chords, and the sounds yet unharmonized, exist, and, last of all, harmony is produced, and first perishes. How, then, will this argument accord with that?"

"Not at all," said Simmias.

"And yet," he said, "if in any argument, there ought to be an accordance in one respecting harmony."

"There ought," said Simmias.

"This of yours, however," he said, "is not in accordance. Consider, then, which of these two statements do you prefer—that knowledge is reminiscence, or the soul harmony?"

"The former by far, Socrates," he replied; "for the latter occurred to me without demonstration, through a certain probability and speciousness whence most men derive their opinions. But I am well aware that arguments which draw their demonstrations from probabilities are idle; and, unless one is on one's guard against them, they are very deceptive, both in geometry and all other subjects. But the argument respecting reminiscence and knowledge may be said to have been demonstrated by a satisfactory hypothesis. For in this way it was said that our soul existed before it came into the body, because the essence that bears the appellation of 'that which is' belongs to it. But of this, as I persuade myself, I am fully and rightly convinced. It is therefore necessary, as it seems, that I should neither allow myself nor anyone else to maintain that the soul is harmony."

"But what, Simmias," said he, "if you consider it thus? Does it appear to you to appertain to harmony, or to any other composition, to subsist in any other way than the very things do of which it is composed?"

"By no means."

84

"And indeed, as I think, neither to do anything, nor suffer anything else, besides what they do or suffer."

He agreed.

"It does not, therefore, appertain to harmony to take the lead of the things of which it is composed, but to follow them."

He assented.

"It is, then, far from being the case that harmony is moved or sends forth sounds contrariwise, or is in any other respect opposed to its parts?"

"Far, indeed," he said.

"What, then? Is not every harmony naturally harmony, so far as it has been made to accord?"

"I do not understand you," he replied.

"Whether," he said, "if it should be in a greater degree and more fully made to accord, supposing that were possible, would the harmony be greater and more full; but if in a less degree and less fully, then would it be inferior and less full?"

"Certainly."

"Is this, then, the case with the soul that, even in the smallest extent, one soul is more fully and in a greater degree, or less fully and in a less degree, this very thing, a soul, than another?"

"In no respect whatever," he replied.

"Well, then," he said, "by Jupiter! is one soul said to possess intelligence and virtue, and to be good, and another folly and vice, and to be bad? and is this said with truth?"

"With truth, certainly."

"Of those, then, who maintain that the soul is harmony, what will anyone say that these things are in the soul, virtue and vice? Will he call them another kind of harmony and discord, and say that the one, the good soul, is harmonized, and, being harmony, contains within itself another harmony, but that the other is discordant, and does not contain within itself another harmony?"

"I am unable to say," replied Simmias; "but it is clear that he who maintains that opinion would say something of the kind."

"But it has been already granted," said he, "that one soul is not more or less a soul than another; and this is an admission that one harmony is not to a greater degree or more fully, or to a less degree or less fully, a harmony, than another; is it not so?"

"Certainly."

"And that that which is neither more or less harmony is neither more nor less harmonized: is it so?"

"It is."

"But does that which is neither more or less harmonized partake of more or less harmony, or an equal amount?"

"An equal amount."

"A soul, therefore, since it is not more or less this very thing, a soul, than another, is not more or less harmonized?"

"Even so."

"Such, then, being its condition, it cannot partake of a greater degree of discord or harmony?"

"Certainly not."

"And, again, such being its condition, can one soul partake of a greater degree of vice or virtue than another, if vice be discord, and virtue harmony?"

"It cannot."

"Or rather, surely, Simmias, according to right reason, no soul will partake of vice, if it is harmony; for doubtless harmony, which is perfectly such, can never partake of discord?"

"Certainly not."

"Neither, therefore, can a soul which is perfectly a soul partake of vice."

"How can it, from what has been already said?"

"From this reasoning, then, all souls of all animals will be equally good, if, at least, they are by nature equally this very thing, souls?"

"It appears so to me, Socrates," he said.

"And does it appear to you," he said, "to have been thus rightly argued, and that the argument would lead to this result, if the hypothesis were correct, that the soul is harmony?"

"On no account whatever," he replied.

"But what," said he, "of all the things that are in man? Is there anything else that you say bears rule except the soul, especially if it be wise?"

"I should say not."

"Whether by yielding to the passions in the body, or by opposing them? My meaning is this: for instance, when heat and thirst are present, by drawing it the contrary way, so as to hinder it from drinking; and when hunger is present, by hindering it from eating; and in ten thousand other instances we see the soul opposing the desires of the body. Do we not?"

"Certainly."

"But have we not before allowed that if the soul were harmony, it would never utter a sound contrary to the tension, relaxation, vibration, or any other affection to which its component parts are subject, but would follow, and never govern them?"

"We did allow it," he replied, "for how could we do otherwise?"

86

"What, then? Does not the soul now appear to act quite the contrary, ruling over all the parts from which anyone might say it subsists, and resisting almost all of them through the whole of life, and exercising dominion over them in all manner of ways; punishing some more severely even with pain, both by gymnastics and medicine, and others more mildly; partly threatening, and partly admonishing the desires, angers and fears, as if, being itself of a different nature, it were conversing with something quite different? Just as Homer has done in the Odyssey,[35] where he speaks of Ulysses—'Having struck his breast, he chid his heart in the following words: Bear up, my heart; ere this thou hast borne far worse.' Do you think that he composed this in the belief that the soul was harmony, and capable of being led by the passions of the body, and not rather that it was able to lead and govern them, as being something much more divine than to be compared with harmony?"

"By Jupiter! Socrates, it appears so to me."

"Therefore, my excellent friend, it is on no account correct for us to say that the soul is a kind of harmony; for, as it appears, we should neither agree with Homer, that divine poet, nor with ourselves."

"Such is the case," he replied.

"Be it so, then," said Socrates, "we have already, as it seems, sufficiently appeased this Theban harmony. But how, Cebes, and by what arguments, shall we appease this Cadmus?"[36]

"You appear to me," replied Cebes, "to be likely to find out; for you have made out this argument against harmony wonderfully beyond my expectation. For when Simmias was saying what his doubts were, I wondered very much whether anyone would be able to answer his reasoning. It, therefore, appeared to me unaccountable that he did not withstand the very first onset of your argument. I should not, therefore, be surprised if the arguments of Cadmus met with the same fate."

"My good friend," said Socrates, "do not speak so boastfully, lest some envious power should overthrow the argument that is about to be urged. These things, however, will be cared for by the deity; but let us, meeting hand to hand, in the manner of Homer, try whether you say anything to the purpose. This, then, is the sum of what you inquire you require it to be proved that our soul is imperishable and immortal; if a philosopher that is about to die, full of confidence and hope that after death he shall be far happier than if he had died after leading a different kind of life, shall not entertain this confidence foolishly and vainly. But to show that the soul is something strong and divine, and that it existed before we men were born, you say not at all hinders, but that all these things may evince, not its immortality, but that the soul is durable, and existed an immense space of time before, and knew and did manythings. But that, for all this, it was not at all the more immortal, but that its very entrance into the body of a man was the beginning of its destruction, as if it were a disease; so that it passes through this life in wretchedness, and at last perishes in that which is called death. But you say that it is of no consequence whether it comes into a body once or often, with respect to our occasion of fear; for it is right he should be afraid, unless he is foolish, who does not know, and cannot give a reason to prove, that the soul is immortal. Such, I think, Cebes, is the sum of what you say; and I purposely repeat it often, that nothing may escape us, and, if you please, you may add to or take from it."

Cebes replied, "I do not wish at present either to take from or add to it; that is what I mean."

Socrates, then having paused for some time, and considered something within himself, said, "You inquire into no easy matter, Cebes; for it is absolutely necessary to discuss the whole question of generation and corruption. If you please, then, I will relate to you what happened to me with reference to them; and afterward, if anything that I shall say shall appear to you useful toward producing conviction on the subject you are now treating of, make use of it."

"I do indeed wish it," replied Cebes.

"Hear my relation, then. When I was a young man, Cebes, I was wonderfully desirous of that wisdom which they call a history of nature; for it appeared to me to be a very sublime thing to know the causes of everything—why each thing is generated, why it perishes, and why it exists. And I often tossed myself upward and downward, considering first such things as these, whether when heat and cold have undergone a certain corruption, as some say, then animals are formed; and whether the blood is that by means of which we think, or air, or fire, or none of these, but that it is the brain that produces the perceptions of hearing, seeing, and smelling; and that from these come memory and opinion; and from memory and opinion, when in a state of rest, in the same way knowledge is produced. And, again, considering the corruptions of these, and the affections incidental to the heavens and the earth, I at length appeared to myself so unskillful in these speculations that nothing could be more so. But I will give you a sufficient proof of this; for I then became, by these very speculations, so very blind with respect to things which I knew clearly before, as it appeared to myself and others, that I unlearned even the things which I thought I knew before, both on many other subjects and also this, why a man grows. For, before, I thought this was evident to everyone—that it proceeds from eating and drinking; for that, when, from the food, flesh is added to flesh, bone to bone, and so on in the same proportion, what is proper to them is added to the several other parts, then the bulk which was small becomes afterward large, and thus that a little man becomes a big one. Such was my opinion at that time. Does it appear to you correct?"

"To me it does," said Cebes.

"Consider this further. I thought that I had formed a right opinion, when, on seeing a tall man standing by a short one, I judged that he was taller by the head, and in like manner, one horse than another; and, still more clearly than this, ten appeared to me to be more than eight by two being added to them, and that two cubits are greater than one cubit by exceeding it a half."

"But now," said Cebes, "what think you of these matters?"

"By Jupiter!" said he, "I am far from thinking that I know the cause of these, for that I cannot even persuade myself of this: when a person has added one to one, whether the one to which the addition has been made has become two, or whether that which has been added, and that to which the addition has been made, have become two by the addition of the one to the other. For I wonder if, when each of these was separate from the other, each was one, and they were not yet two; but when they have approached nearer each other this should be the cause of their becoming two—namely, the union by which they have been placed nearer one another. Nor yet, if any person should divide one, am I able to persuade myself that this, their division, is the cause of its becoming two. For this cause is the contrary to the former one of their becoming two; for then it was because they were brought nearer to each other, and the one was added to the other; but now it is because one is removed and separated from the other. Nor do I yet persuade myself that I know why one is one, nor, in a word, why anything else is produced, or perishes, or exists, according to this method of proceeding; but I mix up another method of my own at random, for this I can on no account give in to."

"But, having once heard a person reading from a book, written, as he said, by Anaxagoras, and which said that it is intelligence that sets in order and is the cause of all things, I was delighted with this cause, and it appeared to me in a manner to be well that intelligence should be the cause of all things, and I considered with myself, if this is so, that the regulating intelligence orders all things, and disposes each in such way as will be best for it. If anyone, then, should desire to discover the cause of everything, in what way it is produced, or perishes, or exists, he must discover this respecting it—in what way it is best for it either to exist, or to suffer, or do anything else. From this mode of reasoning, then, it is proper that a man should consider nothing else, both with respect to himself and others, than what is most excellent and best; and it necessarily follows that this same person must also know that which is worst, for that the knowledge of both of them is the same. Thus reasoning with myself, I was delighted to think I had found in Anaxagoras a preceptor who would instruct me in the causes of things, agreeably to my own mind, and that he would inform me, first, whether the earth is flat or round, and, when he had informed me, would, moreover, explain the cause and necessity of its being so, arguing on the principle of the better, and showing that it is better for it to be such as it is; and if he should say that it is in the middle, that he would, moreover, explain how it is better for it to be in the middle; and if he should make all this clear to me, I was prepared no longer to require any other species of cause. I was in like manner prepared to inquire respecting the sun and moon and the other stars, with respect to their velocities in reference to each other, and their revolutions and other conditions, in what way it is better for both to act and be affected as it does and is. For I never thought that after he had said that these things were set in order by intelligence, he would introduce any other cause for them than that it is best for them to be as they are. Hence, I thought, that in assigning the cause to each of them, and to all in common, he would explain that which is best for each, and the common good of all. And I would not have given up my hopes for a good deal; but, having taken up his books with great eagerness, I read through them as quickly as I could, that I might as soon as possible know the best and the worst."

"From this wonderful hope, however, my friend, I was speedily thrown down, when, as I advance and read over his works, I meet with a man who makes no use of intelligence, nor assigns any causes for the ordering of all things, but makes the causes to consist of air, ether, and water, and many other things equally absurd. And he appeared to me to be very like one who should say that whatever Socrates does he does by intelligence, and then, attempting to describe the causes of each particular action, should say, first of all, that for this reason I am now sitting here, because my body is composed of bones and sinews and that the bones are hard, and have joints separate from each other, but that the sinews, being capable of tension and contraction, cover the bones, together with the flesh and skin which contain them. The bones, therefore, being suspended in their sockets, the nerves, relaxing and tightening, enable me to bend my limbs as I now do, and from this cause I sit here bent up. And if, again, he should assign other similar causes for my conversing with you, assigning as causes voice, and air, and hearing, and ten thousand other things of the kind, omitting to mention the real causes, that since it appeared better to the Athenians to condemn me, I therefore thought it better to sit here, and more just to remain and submit to the punishment which they have ordered; for, by the dog! I think these sinews and bones would have been long ago either in Megara or Boeotia, borne thither by an opinion of that which is best, if I had not thought it more just and honorable to submit to whatever sentence the city might order than to flee and run stealthily away. But to call such things causes is too absurd. But if anyone should say that without possessing such things as bones and sinews, and whatever else I have, I could not do what I pleased, he would speak the truth; but to say that I do as I do through them, and that I act thus by intelligence, and not from the choice of what is best, would be a great and extreme disregard of reason. For this would be not to be able to distinguish that the real cause is one thing, and that another, without which a cause could not be a cause; which, indeed, the generality of men appear to me to do, fumbling, as it were, in the dark, and making use of strange names, so as to denominate them as the very cause. Wherefore one encompassing the earth with a vortex from heaven makes the earth remain fixed; but another, as if it were a broad trough, rests it upon the air as its base; but the power by which these things are now so disposed that they may be placed in the best manner possible, this they neither inquire into, nor do they think that it requires any superhuman strength; but they think they will some time or other find out an Atlas stronger and more immortal than this, and more capable of containing all things; and in reality, the good, and that which ought to hold them together and contain them, they take no account of at all. I, then, should most gladly have become the disciple of anyone who would teach me of such a cause, in what way it is. But when I was disappointed of this, and was neither able to discover it myself, nor to learn it from another, do you wish, Cebes, that I should show you in what way I set out upon a second voyage in search of the cause?"

"I wish it exceedingly," he replied.

"It appeared to me, then," said he, "after this, when I was wearied with considering things that exist, that I ought to beware lest I should suffer in the same way as they do who look at and examine an eclipse of the sun, for some lose the sight of their eyes, unless they behold its image in water, or some similar medium. And I was affected with a similar feeling, and was afraid lest I should be utterly blinded in my soul through beholding things with the eyes, and endeavoring to grasp them by means of the several senses. It seemed to me, therefore, that I ought to have recourse to reasons, and to consider in them the truth of things. Perhaps, however, this similitude of mine may in some respect be incorrect; for I do not altogether admit that he who considers things in their reasons considers them in their images, more than he does who views them in their effects. However, I proceeded thus, and on each occasion laying down the reason, which I deem to be the strongest, whatever things appear to me to accord with this I regard as true, both with respect to the cause and everything else; but such as do not accord I regard as not true. But I wish to explain my meaning to you in a clearer manner; for I think that you do not yet understand me."

"No, by Jupiter!" said Cebes, "not well."

"However," continued he, "I am now saying nothing new, but what I have always at other times, and in a former part of this discussion, never ceased to say. I proceed, then, to attempt to explain to you that species of cause which I have busied myself about, and return again to those well-known subjects, and set out from them, laying down as an hypothesis, that there is a certain abstract beauty, and goodness, and magnitude, and so of all other things; which if you grant me, and allow that they do exist, I hope that I shall be able from these to explain the cause to you, and to discover that the soul is immortal."

"But," said Cebes, "since I grant you this, you may draw your conclusion at once."

"But consider," he said, "what follows from thence, and see if you can agree with me. For it appears to me that if there is anything else beautiful besides beauty itself, it is not beautiful for any other reason than because it partakes of that abstract beauty; and I say the same of everything. Do you admit such a cause?"

"I do admit it," he replied.

"I do not yet understand," he continued, "nor am I able to conceive, those other wise causes; but if anyone should tell me why anything is beautiful, either because it has a blooming florid color, or figure, or anything else of the kind, I dismiss all other reasons, for I am confounded by them all; but I simply, wholly, and perhaps foolishly, confine myself to this, that nothing else causes it to be beautiful except either the presence or communication of that abstract beauty, by whatever means and in whatever way communicated; for I cannot yet affirm this with certainty, but only that by means of beauty all beautiful things become beautiful. For this appears to me the safest answer to give both to myself and others; and adhering to this, I think that I shall never fall, but that it is a safe answer both for me and anyone else to give—that by means of beauty beautiful things become beautiful. Does it not also seem so to you?"

"It does."

"And that by magnitude great things become great, and greater things, greater; and by littleness less things become less?"

"Yes."

You would not, then, approve of it, if anyone said that one person is greater than another by the head, and that the less is less by the very same thing; but you would maintain that you mean nothing else than that everything that is greater than another is greater by nothing else than magnitude, and that it is greater on this account—that is, on account of magnitude; and that the less is less by nothing else than littleness, and on this account less—that is, on account of littleness; being afraid, I think, lest some opposite argument should meet you if

92

you should say that anyone is greater and less by the head; as, first, that the greater is greater, and the less less, by the very same thing; and, next, that the greater is greater by the head, which is small; and that it is monstrous to suppose that anyone is great through something small. Should you not be afraid of this?"

To which said Cebes, smilingly, "Indeed, I should."

"Should you not, then," he continued, "be afraid to say that ten is more than eight by two, and for this cause exceeds it, and not by number, and on account of number? and that two cubits are greater than one cubit by half, and not by magnitude (for the fear is surely the same)?"

"Certainly," he replied.

"What, then? When one has been added to one, would you not beware of saying that the addition is the cause of its being two, or division when it has been divided; and would you not loudly assert that you know no other way in which each thing subsists, than by partaking of the peculiar essence of each of which it partakes, and that in these cases you can assign no other cause of its becoming two than its partaking of duality; and that such things as are to become two must needs partake of this, and what is to become one, of unity; but these divisions and additions, and other such subtleties, you would dismiss, leaving them to be given as answers by persons wiser than yourself; whereas you, fearing, as it is said, your own shadow and inexperience, would adhere to this safe hypothesis, and answer accordingly? But if anyone should assail this hypothesis of yours, would you not dismiss him, and refrain from answering him till you had considered the consequences resulting from it, whether in your opinion they agree with or differ from each other? But when it should be necessary for you to give a reason for it, would you give one in a similar way, by again laying down another hypothesis, which should appear the best of higher principles, until you arrived at something satisfactory; but, at the same time, you would avoid making confusion, as disputants do, in treating of the first principle and the results arising from it, if you really desire to arrive at the truth of things? For they, perhaps, make no account at all of this, nor pay any attention to it; for they are able, through their wisdom, to mingle all things together, and at the same time please themselves. But you, if you are a philosopher, would act, I think, as I now describe."

"You speak most truly," said Simmias and Cebes together.

Echec. By Jupiter! Phædo, they said so with good reason; for he appears to me to have explained these things with wonderful clearness, even to one endued with a small degree of intelligence.

Phaedo. Certainly, Echecrates, and so it appeared to all who were present.

Echec. And so it appears to me, who was absent, and now hear it related. But what was said after this?

As well as I remember, when these things had been granted him, and it was allowed that each several idea exists of itself,[37] and that other things partaking of them receive their denomination from them, he next asked: "If, then," he said, "you admit that things are so, whether, when you say that Simmias is greater than Socrates, but less than Phædo, do you not then say that magnitude and littleness are both in Simmias?"

"I do."

"And yet," he said, "you must confess that Simmias's exceeding Socrates is not actually true in the manner in which the words express it; for Simmias does not naturally exceed Socrates in that he is Simmias, but in consequence of the magnitude which he happens to have; nor, again, does he exceed Socrates because Socrates is Socrates, but because Socrates possesses littleness in comparison with his magnitude?"

"True."

"Nor, again, is Simmias exceeded by Phædo, because Phædo is Phædo, but because Phædo possesses magnitude in comparison with Simmias's littleness?"

"It is so."

"Thus, then, Simmias has the appellation of being both little and great, being between both, by exceeding the littleness of one through his own magnitude, and to the other yielding a magnitude that exceeds his own littleness." And at the same time, smiling, he said, "I seem to speak with the precision of a short-hand writer; however, it is as I say."

He allowed it.

"But I say it for this reason, wishing you to be of the same opinion as myself. For it appears to me, not only that magnitude itself is never disposed to be at the same time great and little, but that magnitude in us never admits the little nor is disposed to be exceeded, but one of two things, either to flee and withdraw when its contrary, the little, approaches it, or, when it has actually come, to perish; but that it is not disposed, by sustaining and receiving littleness, to be different from what it was. Just as I, having received and sustained littleness, and still continuing the person that I am, am this same little person; but that, while it is great, never endures to be little. And, in like manner, the little that is in us is not disposed at any time to become or to be great, nor is anything else among contraries, while it continues what it was, at the same time disposed to become and to be its contrary; but in this contingency it either departs or perishes."

"It appears so to me," said Cebes, "in every respect."

But someone of those present, on hearing this, I do not clearly remember who he was, said, "By the gods! was not the very contrary of what is now asserted admitted in the former part of our discussion, that the greater is produced from the less, and the less from the greater, and, in a word, that the very production of contraries is from contraries? But now it appears to me to be asserted that this can never be the case."

Upon this Socrates, having leaned his head forward and listened, said, "You have reminded me in a manly way; you do not, however, perceive the difference between what is now and what was then asserted. For then it was said that a contrary thing is produced from a contrary; but now, that a contrary can never become contrary to itself—neither that which is in us, nor that which is in nature. For then, my friend, we spoke of things that have contraries, calling them by the appellation of those things; but now we are speaking of those very things from the presence of which things so called receive their appellation, and of these very things we say that they are never disposed to admit of production from each other." And, at the same time looking at Cebes, "Has anything that has been said, Cebes, disturbed you?"

"Indeed," said Cebes, "I am not at all so disposed; however, I by no means say that there are not manythings that disturb me."

"Then," he continued, "we have quite agreed to this, that a contrary can never be contrary to itself."

"Most certainly," he replied.

"But, further," he said, "consider whether you will agree with me in this also. Do you call heat and cold anything?"

"I do."

"The same as snow and fire?"

"By Jupiter! I do not."

"But heat is something different from fire, and cold something different from snow?"

"Yes."

"But this, I think, is apparent to you—that snow, while it is snow, can never, when it has admitted heat, as we said before, continue to be what it was, snow and hot; but, on the approach of heat, it must either withdraw or perish?"

"Certainly."

"And, again, that fire, when cold approaches it, must either depart or perish; but that it will never endure, when it has admitted coldness, to continue what it was, fire and cold?"

"You speak truly," he said.

"It happens, then," he continued, "with respect to some of such things, that not only is the idea itself always thought worthy of the same appellation, but likewise something else which is not, indeed, that idea itself, but constantly retains its form so long as it exists. What I mean will perhaps be clearer in the following examples: the odd in number must always possess the name by which we now call it, must it not?"

"Certainly."

"Must it alone, of all things—for this I ask—or is there anything else which is not the same as the odd, but yet which we must always call odd, together with its own name, because it is so constituted by nature that it can never be without the odd? But this, I say, is the case with the number three, and many others. For consider with respect to the number three: does it not appear to you that it must always be called by its own name, as well as by that of the odd, which is not the same as the number three? Yet such is the nature of the number three, five, and the entire half of number, that though they are not the same as the odd, yet each of them is always odd. And, again, two and four, and the whole other series of number, though not the same as the even, are nevertheless each of them always even: do you admit this, or not?"

"How should I not?" he replied.

"Observe then," said he, "what I wish to prove. It is this—that it appears not only that these contraries do not admit each other, but that even such things as are not contrary to each other, and yet always possess contraries, do not appear to admit that idea which is contrary to the idea that exists in themselves, but, when it approaches, perish or depart. Shall we not allow that the number three would first perish, and suffer anything whatever, rather than endure, while it is still three, to become even?"

"Most certainly," said Cebes.

"And yet," said he, "the number two is not contrary to three."

"Surely not."

"Not only, then, do ideas that are contrary never allow the approach of each other, but some other things also do not allow the approach of contraries."

"You say very truly," he replied.

"Do you wish, then," he said, "that, if we are able, we should define what these things are?"

"Certainly."

"Would they not then, Cebes," he said, "be such things as, whatever they occupy, compel that thing not only to retain its own idea, but also that of something which is always a contrary?"

"How do you mean?"

"As we just now said. For you know, surely, that whatever things the idea of three occupies must of necessity not only be three, but also odd?"

"Certainly."

"To such a thing, then, we assert, that the idea contrary to that form which constitutes this can never come."

"It cannot."

"But did the odd make it so?"

"Yes."

"And is the contrary to this the idea of the even?"

"Yes."

"The idea of the even, then, will never come to the three?"

"No, surely."

"Three, then, has no part in the even?"

"None whatever."

"The number three is uneven?"

"Yes."

"What, therefore, I said should be defined—namely, what things they are which, though not contrary to some particular thing, yet do not admit of the contrary itself; as, in the present instance, the number three, though not contrary to the even, does not any the more admit it, for it always brings the contrary with it, just as the number two does to the odd, fire to cold, and many other particulars. Consider, then, whether you would thus define, not only that a contrary does not admit a contrary, but also that that which brings with it a contrary to that to which it approaches will never admit the contrary of that which it brings with it. But call it to mind again, for it will not be useless to hear it often repeated. Five will not admit the idea of the even, nor ten, its double, that of the odd. This double, then, though it is itself contrary to something else,[38] yet will not admit the idea of the odd, nor will half as much again, nor other things of the kind, such as the half and the third part, admit the idea of the whole, if you follow me, and agree with me that it is so."

"I entirely agree with you," he said, "and follow you."

"Tell me again, then," he said, "from the beginning; and do not answer me in the terms in which I put the question, but in different ones, imitating my example. For I say this because, besides that safe mode of answering which I mentioned at first,[39] from what has now been said, I see another no less safe one. For if you should ask me what that is which, if it be in the body, will cause it to be hot, I should not give you that safe but unlearned answer, that it is heat, but one more elegant, from what we have just now said, that it is fire; nor, if you should ask what that is which, if it be in the body, will cause it to be diseased, should I say that it is disease, but fever; nor if you should ask what that is which, if it be in number, will cause it to be odd, should I say that it is unevenness, but

97

unity; and so with other things. But consider whether you sufficiently understand what I mean."

"Perfectly so," he replied.

"Answer me, then," he said, "what that is which, when it is in the body, the body will be alive?"

"Soul," he replied.

"Is not this, then, always the case?"

"How should it not be?" said he.

"Does the soul, then, always bring life to whatever it occupies?"

"It does indeed," he replied.

"Whether, then, is there anything contrary to life or not?"

"There is," he replied.

"What?"

"Death."

"The soul, then, will never admit the contrary of that which it brings with it, as has been already allowed?"

"Most assuredly," replied Cebes.

"What, then? How do we denominate that which does not admit the idea of the even?"

"Uneven," he replied.

"And that which does not admit the just, nor the musical?"

"Unmusical," he said, "and unjust."

"Be it so. But what do we call that which does not admit death?"

"Immortal," he replied.

"Therefore, does not the soul admit death?"

"No."

"Is the soul, then, immortal?"

"Immortal."

"Be it so," he said. "Shall we say, then, that this has been now demonstrated? or how think you?"

"Most completely, Socrates."

"What, then," said he, "Cebes, if it were necessary for the uneven to be imperishable, would the number three be otherwise than imperishable?"

"How should it not?"

"If, therefore, it were also necessary that what is without heat should be imperishable, when anyone should introduce heat to snow, would not the snow withdraw itself, safe and unmelted? For it would not perish; nor yet would it stay and admit the heat."

"You say truly," he replied.

"In like manner, I think, if that which is insusceptible of cold were imperishable, that when anything cold approached the fire, it would neither be extinguished nor perish, but would depart quite safe."

"Of necessity," he said.

"Must we not, then, of necessity," he continued, "speak thus of that which is immortal? if that which is immortal is imperishable, it is impossible for the soul to perish, when death approaches it. For, from what has been said already, it will not admit death, nor will ever be dead; just as we said that three will never be even, nor, again, will the odd; nor will fire be cold, nor yet the heat that is in fire. But someone may say, what hinders, though the odd can never become even by the approach of the even, as we have allowed, yet, when the odd is destroyed, that the even should succeed in its place? We could not contend with him who should make this objection that it is not destroyed, for the uneven is not imperishable; since, if this were granted us, we might easily have contended that, on the approach of the even, the odd and the three depart; and we might have contended in the same way with respect to fire, heat, and the rest, might we not?"

"Certainly."

"Wherefore, with respect to the immortal, if we have allowed that it is imperishable, the soul, in addition to its being immortal, must also be imperishable; if not, there will be need of other arguments."

"But there is no need," he said, "so far as that is concerned; for scarcely could anything not admit of corruption, if that which is immortal and eternal is liable to it."

"The deity, indeed, I think," said Socrates, "and the idea itself of life, and if anything else is immortal, must be allowed by all beings to be incapable of dissolution."

"By Jupiter!" he replied, "by all men, indeed, and still more, as I think, by the gods."

"Since, then, that which is immortal is also incorruptible, can the soul, since it is immortal, be anything else than imperishable?"

"It must, of necessity, be so."

"When, therefore, death approaches a man, the mortal part of him, as it appears, dies, but the immortal part departs safe and uncorrupted, having withdrawn itself from death?"

"It appears so."

"The soul, therefore," he said, "Cebes, is most certainly immortal and imperishable, and our souls will really exist in Hades."

"Therefore, Socrates," he said, "I have nothing further to say against this, nor any reason for doubting your arguments. But if Simmias here, or anyone else, has anything to say, it were well for him not to be silent; for I know not to what other opportunity beyond the present anyone can defer it, who wishes either to speak or hear about these things."

"But, indeed," said Simmias, "neither have I any reason to doubt what has been urged; yet, from the magnitude of the subject discussed, and from my low opinion of human weakness, I am compelled still to retain a doubt within myself with respect to what has been said."

"Not only so, Simmias," said Socrates, "but you say this well; and, moreover, the first hypotheses, even though they are credible to you, should nevertheless be examined more carefully; and if you should investigate them sufficiently, I think you will follow my reasoning as far as it is possible for man to do so; and if this very point becomes clear, you will inquire no further."

"You speak truly," he said.

"But it is right, my friends," he said, "that we should consider this—- that if the soul is immortal, it requires our care not only for the present time, which we call life, but for all time; and the danger would now appear to be dreadful if one should neglect it. For if death were a deliverance from everything, it would be a great gain for the wicked, when they die, to be delivered at the same time from the body, and from their vices together with the soul; but now, since it appears to be immortal, it can have no other refuge from evils, nor safety, except by becoming as good and wise as possible. For the soul goes to Hades possessing nothing else than its discipline and education, which are said to be of the greatest advantage or detriment to the dead, on the very beginning of his journey thither. For, thus, it is said that each person's demon who was assigned to him while living, when he dies conducts him to some place, where they that are assembled together must receive sentence, and then proceed to Hades with that guide who has been ordered to conduct them from hence thither. But there having received their deserts, and having remained the appointed time, another guide brings them back hither again, after many and long revolutions of time. The journey, then, is not such as the Telephus of Æschylus describes it; for he says that a simple path leads to Hades; but it appears to me to be neither simple nor one, for there would be no need of guides, nor could anyone ever miss the way, if there were but one. But now it appears to have many divisions and windings; and this I conjecture from our religious and funeral rites.[40] The well-ordered and wise soul, then, both follows, and is not ignorant of its present condition; but that which through passion clings to the body, as I said before, having longingly fluttered about it for a long time, and about its visible place,[41] after vehement resistance and great suffering, is forcibly and with great difficulty led away by its appointed demon. And when it arrives at the place where the others are, impure and having done any such thing as the committal of unrighteous murders or other similar actions, which are kindred to these, and are the deeds of kindred souls, everyone shuns it and turns away from it, and will be neither its fellow-traveler nor guide; but it wanders about, oppressed with every kind of helplessness, until certain periods have elapsed; and when these are completed, it is carried, of necessity, to an abode suitable to it. But the soul which has passed through life with purity and moderation, having obtained the gods for its fellow-travelers and guides, settles each in the place suited to it. There are, indeed, many and wonderful places in the earth, and it is itself neither of such a kind nor of such a magnitude as is supposed by those who are accustomed to speak of the earth, as I have been persuaded by a certain person."

Whereupon Simmias said, "How mean you, Socrates? For I, too, have heard manythings about the earth—not, however, those things which have obtained your belief. I would, therefore, gladly hear them."

"Indeed, Simmias, the art of Glaucus[42] does not seem to me to be required to relate what these things are. That they are true, however, appears to me more than the art of Glaucus can prove, and, besides, I should probably not be able to do it; and even if I did know how, what remains to me of life, Simmias, seems insufficient for the length of the subject. However, the form of the earth, such as I am persuaded it is, and the different places in it, nothing hinders me from telling."

"But that will be enough," said Simmias.

"I am persuaded, then," said he, "in the first place, that, if the earth is in the middle of the heavens, and is of a spherical form, it has no need of air, nor of any other similar force, to prevent it from falling; but that the similarity of the heavens to themselves on every side, and the equilibrium of the earth itself, are sufficient to support it; for a thing in a state of equilibrium when placed in the middle of something that presses it equally on all sides cannot incline more or less on any side, but, being equally affected all around, remains unmoved. In the first place, then," he said, "I am persuaded of this."

"And very properly so," said Simmias.

"Yet, further," said he, "that it is very large, and that we who inhabit some small portion of it, from the river Phasis to the pillars of Hercules, dwell about the sea, like ants or frogs about a marsh; and that many others elsewhere dwell in many similar places, for that there are everywhere about the earth many hollows of various forms and sizes into which there is a confluence of water, mist and air; but that the earth itself, being pure, is situated in the pure heavens, in which are the stars, and which most persons who are accustomed to speak about such things call ether; of which these things are the sediment, and are continually flowing into the hollow parts of the earth. That we are ignorant, then, that we are dwelling in its hollows, and imagine that we inhabit the upper parts of the earth, just as if anyone dwelling in the bottom of the sea should think that he dwelt on the sea, and, beholding the sun and the other stars through the water, should imagine that the sea was the heavens; but, through sloth and weakness, should never have reached the surface of the sea; nor, having emerged and risen up from the sea to this region, have seen how much more pure and more beautiful it is than the place where he is, nor has heard of it from anyone else who has seen it. This, then, is the very condition in which we are; for, dwelling in some hollow of the earth, we think that we dwell on the surface of it, and call the air heaven, as if the stars moved through this, being heaven itself. But this is because, by reason of our weakness and sloth, we are unable to reach to the summit of the air. Since, if anyone could arrive at its summit, or, becoming winged, could fly up thither, or, emerging from hence, he would see—just as with us, fishes, emerging from the sea, behold what is here, so anyone would behold the things there; and if his nature were able to endure the contemplation, he would know that that is the true heaven, and the true light, and the true earth. For this earth and these stones, and the whole region here, are decayed and corroded, as things in the sea by the saltness; for nothing of any value grows in the sea, nor, in a word, does it contain anything perfect; but there are caverns and sand, and mud in abundance, and filth, in whatever parts of the sea there is earth, nor are they at all worthy to be compared with the beautiful things with us. But, on the other hand, those things in the upper regions of the earth would appear far more to excel the things with us. For, if we may tell a beautiful fable, it is well worth hearing, Simmias, what kind the things are on the earth beneath the heavens."

"Indeed, Socrates," said Simmias, "we should be very glad to hear that fable."

"First of all, then, my friend," he continued, "this earth, if anyone should survey it from above, is said to have the appearance of balls covered with twelve different pieces of leather, variegated and distinguished with colors, of which the colors found here, and which painters use, are, as it were, copies. But there the whole earth is composed of such, and far more brilliant and pure than these; for one part of it is purple, and of wonderful beauty, part of a golden color, and part of white, more white than chalk or snow, and, in like manner, composed of other colors, and those more in number and more beautiful than any we have ever beheld. And those very hollow parts of the earth, though filled with water and air, exhibit a certain species of color, shining among the variety of other colors, so that one continually variegated aspect presents itself to the view. In this earth, being such, all things that grow, grow in a manner proportioned to its nature—trees, flowers and fruits; and, again, in like manner, its mountains and stones

102

possess, in the same proportion, smoothness and transparency, and more beautiful colors; of which the well-known stones here that are so highly prized are but fragments, such as sardine-stones, jaspers, and emeralds, and all of that kind. But there, there is nothing subsists that is not of this character, and even more beautiful than these. But the reason of this is, because the stones there are pure, and not eaten up and decayed, like those here, by rottenness and saltness, which flow down hither together, and which produce deformity and disease in the stones and the earth, and in other things, even animals and plants. But that earth is adorned with all these, and, moreover, with gold and silver, and other things of the kind: for they are naturally conspicuous, being numerous and large, and in all parts of the earth; so that to behold it is a sight for the blessed. There are also many other animals and men upon it, some dwelling in mid-earth, others about the air, as we do about the sea, and others in islands which the air flows round, and which are near the continent; and, in one word, what water and the sea are to us, for our necessities, the air is to them; and what air is to us, that ether is to them. But their seasons are of such a temperament that they are free from disease, and live for a much longer time than those here, and surpass us in sight, hearing, and smelling, and everything of this kind, as much as air excels water, and ether air, in purity. Moreover, they have abodes and temples of the gods, in which gods really dwell, and voices and oracles, and sensible visions of the gods, and such-like intercourse with them; the sun, too, and moon, and stars, are seen by them such as they really are, and their felicity in other respects is correspondent with these things."

"And, such, indeed, is the nature of the whole earth, and the parts about the earth; but there are many places all round it throughout its cavities, some deeper and more open than that in which we dwell; but others that are deeper have a less chasm than our region, and others are shallower in depth than it is here, and broader. But all these are in many places perforated one into another under the earth, some with narrower and some with wider channels, and have passages through, by which a great quantity of water flows from one into another, as into basins, and there are immense bulks of ever-flowing rivers under the earth, both of hot and cold water, and a great quantity of fire, and mighty rivers of fire, and many of liquid mire, some purer, and some more miry, as in Sicily there are rivers of mud that flow before the lava, and the lava itself, and from these the several places are filled, according as the overflow from time to time happens to come to each of them. But all these move up and down, as it were, by a certain oscillation existing in the earth. And this oscillation proceeds from such natural cause as this; one of the chasms of the earth is exceedingly large, and perforated through the entire earth, and is that which Homer[43] speaks of, 'very far off, where is the most profound abyss beneath the earth,' which elsewhere both he and many other poets have called Tartarus. For into this chasm all rivers flow together, and from it flow out again; but they severally derive their character from the earth through which they flow. And the reason why all streams flow out from thence, and flow into it, is because this liquid has neither bottom nor base. Therefore, it oscillates and fluctuates up and down, and the air and the wind around it do the same; for they accompany it both when it rushes to those parts of the earth, and when to these. And as in respiration the flowing breath is continually breathed out and drawn in, so there the wind oscillating with the liquid causes certain vehement and irresistible winds both as it enters and goes out. When, therefore, the water rushing in descends to the place which we call the lower region, it flows through the earth into the streams there, and fills them, just as men pump up water. But when again it leaves those regions and rushes hither, it again fills the rivers here; and these, when filled, flow through channels and through the earth, and, having severally reached the several places to which they are journeying, they make seas, lakes, rivers, and fountains. Then, sinking again from thence beneath the earth, some of them having gone round longer and more numerous places, and others round fewer and shorter, they again discharge themselves into Tartarus—some much lower than they were drawn up, others only a little so; but all of them flow in again beneath the point at which they flowed out. And some issue out directly opposite the place by which they flow in, others on the same side. There are also some which, having gone round altogether in a circle, folding themselves once or several times round the earth, like serpents, when they have descended as low as possible, discharge themselves again; and it is possible for them to descend on either side as far as the middle, but not beyond; for in each direction there is an acclivity to the streams both ways."

"Now, there are many other large and various streams; but among this great number there are four certain streams, of which the largest, and that which flows most outwardly round the earth, is called Ocean; but directly opposite this, and flowing in a contrary direction, is Acheron, which flows through other desert places, and, moreover, passing under the earth, reaches the Acherusian lake, where the souls of most who die arrive; and, having remained there for certain destined periods, some longer and some shorter, are again sent forth into the generations of animals. A third river issues midway between these, and, near its source, falls into a vast region, burning with abundance of fire, and forms a lake larger than our sea, boiling with water and mud. From hence it proceeds in a circle, turbulent and muddy, and, folding itself round it, reaches both other places and the extremity of the Acherusian lake, but does not mingle with its water; but, folding itself oftentimes beneath the earth, it discharges itself into the lower parts of Tartarus. And this is the river which they call Pyriphlegethon, whose burning streams emit dissevered fragments in whatever part of the earth they happen to be. Opposite to this, again, the fourth river first falls into a place dreadful and savage, as it is said, having its whole color like cyanus:[44] this they call Stygian, and the lake which the river forms by its discharge, Styx. This river, having fallen in here, and received awful power in the water, sinking beneath the earth, proceeds, folding itself round, in an opposite course to Pyriphlegethon, and meets it in the Acherusian lake from, a contrary direction. Neither does the water of this river mingle with any other; but it, too, having gone round in a circle, discharges itself into Tartarus, opposite to Pyriphlegethon. Its name, as the poets say, is Cocytus."

"These things being thus constituted, when the dead arrive at the place to which their demon leads them severally, first of all they are judged, as well those who have lived well and piously, as those who have not. And those who appear to have passed a middle kind of life, proceeding to Acheron, and embarking in the vessels they have, on these arrive at the lake, and there dwell; and when they are purified, and have suffered punishment for the iniquities they may have committed, they are set free, and each receives the reward of his good deeds, according to his deserts. But those who appear to be incurable, through the magnitude of their offenses, either from having committed many and great sacrileges, or many unjust and lawless murders, or other similar crimes, these a suitable destiny hurls into Tartarus, whence they never come forth. But those who appear to have been guilty of curable yet great offenses—such as those who, through anger, have committed any violence against father or mother, and have lived the remainder of their life in a state of penitence, or they who have become homicides in a similar manner—these must, of necessity, fall into Tartarus. But after they have fallen, and have been there for a year, the wave casts them forth, the homicides into Cocytus, but the parricides and matricides into Pyriphlegethon. But when, being borne along, they arrive at the Acherusian lake, there they cry out to and invoke, some those whom they slew, others those whom they injured, and, invoking them, they entreat and implore them to suffer them to go out into the lake, and to receive them, and if they persuade them, they go out, and are freed from their sufferings, but if not, they are borne back to Tartarus, and thence again to the rivers. And they do not cease from suffering this until they have persuaded those whom they have injured, for this sentence was imposed on them by the judges. But those who are found to have lived an eminently holy life, these are they who, being freed and set at large from these regions in the earth as from a prison, arrive at the pure abode above, and dwell on the upper parts of the earth. And among these, they who have sufficiently purified themselves by philosophy shall live without bodies, throughout all future time, and shall arrive at habitations yet more beautiful than these which it is neither easy to describe, nor at present is there sufficient time for the purpose."

"But, for the sake of these things which we have described, we should use every endeavor, Simmias, so as to acquire virtue and wisdom in this life, for the reward is noble, and the hope great."

"To affirm positively, indeed, that these things are exactly as I have described them does not become a man of sense. That, however, either this, or something of the kind, takes place with respect to our souls and their habitations—since our soul is certainly immortal—this appears to me most fitting to be believed, and worthy the hazard for one who trusts in its reality; for the hazard is noble, and it is right to allure ourselves with such things, as with enchantments, for which reason I have prolonged my story to such a length. On account of these things, then, a man ought to be confident about his soul who, during this life, has disregarded all the pleasures and ornaments of the body as foreign from his nature, and who, having thought that they do more harm than good, has zealously applied himself to the acquirement of knowledge, and who, having adorned his soul, not with a foreign, but its own proper ornament—temperance, justice, fortitude, freedom, and truth—thus waits for his passage to Hades, as one who is ready to depart whenever destiny shall summon him. You, then," he continued, "Simmias and Cebes, and the rest, will each of you depart at some future time, but now destiny summons me, as a tragic writer would say, and it is nearly time for me to betake myself to the bath, for it appears to me to be better to drink the poison after I have bathed myself, and not to trouble the women with washing my dead body."

When he had thus spoken, Crito said, "So be it, Socrates, but what commands have you to give to these or to me, either respecting your children, or any other matter, in attending to which we can most oblige you?"

"What I always say, Crito," he replied, "nothing new that by taking care of yourselves you will oblige both me and mine, and yourselves, whatever you do, though you should not now promise it, and if you neglect yourselves, and will not live, as it were, in the footsteps of what has been now and formerly said, even though you should promise much at present, and that earnestly, you will do no good at all."

"We will endeavor, then, so to do," he said. "But how shall we bury you?"

"Just as you please," he said, "if only you can catch me, and I do not escape from you." And, at the same time smiling gently, and looking round on us, he said, "I cannot persuade Crito, my friends, that I am that Socrates who is now conversing with you, and who methodizes each part of the discourse; but he thinks that I am he whom he will shortly behold dead, and asks how he should bury me. But that which I some time since argued at length, that when I have drunk the poison I shall no longer remain with you, but shall depart to some happy state of the blessed, this I seem to have urged to him in vain, though I meant at the same time to console both you and myself. Be ye, then, my sureties to Crito," he said, "in an obligation contrary to that which he made to the judges (for he undertook that I should remain); but do you be sureties that, when I die, I shall not remain, but shall depart, that Crito may more easily bear it; and, when he sees my body either burned or buried, may not be afflicted for me, as if I suffered from some dreadful thing; nor say at my interment that Socrates is laid out, or is carried out, or is buried. For be well assured," he said, "most excellent Crito, that to speak improperly is not only culpable as to the thing itself, but likewise occasions some injury to our souls. You must have a good courage, then, and say that you bury my body, and bury it in such a manner as is pleasing to you, and as you think is most agreeable to our laws."

When he had said thus, he rose, and went into a chamber to bathe, and Crito followed him, but he directed us to wait for him. We waited, therefore, conversing among ourselves about what had been said, and considering it again, and sometimes speaking about our calamity, how severe it would be to us, sincerely thinking that, like those who are deprived of a father, we should pass the rest of our life as orphans. When he had bathed, and his children were brought to him (for he had two little sons and one grown up), and the women belonging to his family were come, having conversed with them in the presence of Crito, and given them such injunctions as he wished, he directed the women and children to go away, and then returned to us. And it was now near sunset; for he spent a considerable time within. But when he came from bathing he sat down, and did not speak much afterward; then the officer of the Eleven came in, and, standing near him, said, "Socrates, I shall not have to find that fault with you that I do with others, that they are angry with me, and curse me, when, by order of the archons, I bid them drink the poison. But you, on all other occasions during the time you have been here, I have found to be the most noble, meek, and excellent man of all that ever came into this place; and, therefore, I am now well convinced that you will not be angry with me (for you know who are to blame), but with them. Now, then (for you know what I came to announce to you), farewell, and endeavor to bear what is inevitable as easily as possible." And at the same time, bursting into tears, he turned away and withdrew.

And Socrates, looking after him, said, "And thou, too, farewell. We will do as you direct." At the same time turning to us, he said, "How courteous the man is!

During the whole time I have been here he has visited me, and conversed with me sometimes, and proved the worthiest of men; and now how generously he weeps for me! But come, Crito, let us obey him, and let someone bring the poison, if it is ready pounded; but if not, let the man pound it."

Then Crito said, "But I think, Socrates, that the sun is still on the mountains, and has not yet set. Besides, I know that others have drunk the poison very late, after it had been announced to them, and have supped and drunk freely, and some even have enjoyed the objects of their love. Do not hasten, then, for there is yet time."

Upon this Socrates replied, "These men whom you mention, Crito, do these things with good reason, for they think they shall gain by so doing; and I, too, with good reason, shall not do so; for I think I shall gain nothing by drinking a little later, except to become ridiculous to myself, in being so fond of life, and sparing of it, when none any longer remains. Go then," he said, "obey, and do not resist."

Crito, having heard this, nodded to the boy that stood near. And the boy, having gone out and staid for some time, came, bringing with him the man that was to administer the poison, who brought it ready pounded in a cup. And Socrates, on seeing the man, said, "Well, my good friend, as you are skilled in these matters, what must I do?"

"Nothing else," he replied, "than, when you have drunk it, walk about until there is a heaviness in your legs; then lie down: thus it will do its purpose." And at the same time he held out the cup to Socrates. And he having received it very cheerfully, Echecrates neither trembling, nor changing at all in color or countenance, but, as he was wont, looking steadfastly at the man, said, "What say you of this potion, with respect to making a libation to anyone, is it lawful or not?"

"We only pound so much, Socrates," he said, "as we think sufficient to drink."

"I understand you," he said; "but it is certainly both lawful and right to pray to the gods, that my departure hence thither may be happy; which, therefore, I pray, and so may it be." And as he said this, he drank it off readily and calmly. Thus far, most of us were with difficulty able to restrain ourselves from weeping; but when we saw him drinking, and having finished the draught, we could do so no longer; but, in spite of myself, the tears came in full torrent, so that, covering my face, I wept for myself; for I did not weep for him, but for my own fortune, in being deprived of such a friend. But Crito, even before me, when he could not restrain his tears, had risen up. But Apollodorus, even before this, had not ceased weeping; and then, bursting into an agony of grief, weeping and lamenting, he pierced the heart of everyone present, except Socrates himself. But he said,

"What are you doing, my admirable friends? I, indeed, for this reason chiefly, sent away the women, that they might not commit any folly of this kind. For I have heard that it is right to die with good omens. Be quiet, therefore, and bear up."

When we heard this, we were ashamed, and restrained our tears. But he, having walked about, when he said that his legs were growing heavy, lay down on his back; for the man had so directed him. And, at the same time, he who gave the poison taking hold of him, after a short interval, examined his feet and legs; and then, having pressed his foot hard, he asked if he felt it: he said that he did not. And after this he pressed his thighs; and, thus going higher, he showed us that he was growing cold and stiff. Then Socrates touched himself, and said that when the poison reached his heart he should then depart. But now the parts around the lower belly were almost cold; when, uncovering himself, for he had been covered over, he said (and they were his last words), "Crito, we owe a cock to Aesculapius; pay it, therefore; and do not neglect it."

"It shall be done," said Crito; "but consider whether you have anything else to say."

To this question he gave no reply; but, shortly after, he gave a convulsive movement, and the man covered him, and his eyes were fixed; and Crito, perceiving it, closed his mouth and eyes.

This, Echecrates, was the end of our friend,—a man, as we may say, the best of all of his time that we have known, and, moreover, the most wise and just.

Footnotes

[25] Phlius, to which Echecrates belonged, was a town of Sicyonia, in Peloponnesus.

[26] A Pythagorean of Crotona.

[27] Namely, "that it is better to die than to live."

[28] Hitto, Boetian for hioto.

[29] Of Pythagoras.

[30] Some boyish spirit.

[31] That is, at a time of life when the body is in full vigor.

[32] In the original there is a play on the words Haides and   haeides, which I can only attempt to retain by departing from   the usual rendering of the former word.

[33] By this I understand him to mean that the soul alone can perceive   the truth, but the senses, as they are different, receive and convey   different

impressions of the same thing; thus, the eye receives one   impression of an object, the ear a totally different one.

[34] kai ahythis eteros kai eteros, that is, "with one argument   after another" Though Cousin translates it et successivement tout   different de luimeme and Ast, et rursus alia atque alia, which   may be taken in either sense, yet it appears to me to mean that,   when a man repeatedly discovers the fallacy of arguments which he   before believed to be true, he distrusts reasoning altogether, just   as one who meets with friend after friend who proves unfaithful   becomes a misanthrope.

[35] Lib. xx, v. 7.

[36] Harmony was the wife of Cadmus, the founder of Thebes; Socrates, therefore, compares his two Theban friends, Simmias and Cebes, with them, and says that, having overcome Simmias, the advocate of   Harmony, he must now deal with Cebes, who is represented by Cadmus.

[37] einai ti, literally, "is something."

[38] That is, to single.

[39] Sec. 113.

[40] It is difficult to express the distinction between osia   and nomima. The former word seems to have reference to the souls of   the dead; the latter, to their bodies.

[41] Its place of interment.

[42] A proverb meaning "a matter of great difficulty."

[43] "Iliad," lib. viii., v. 14.

[44] A metallic substance of a deep-blue color, frequently mentioned by   the earliest Grecian writers, but of which the nature is unknown.

Made in the USA
Middletown, DE
18 March 2023